In the Boardroom & Beyond: Quotes to Drive Business Success

USAMA BAJWA

DANISH ALI BAJWA

Copyright © 2023 by RK Books

All rights reserved.

No part of this publication may be reproduced, distributed, or transmitted in any form or by any means, including photocopying, recording, or other electronic or mechanical methods, without the prior written permission of the publisher, except in the case of brief quotations embodied in critical reviews and certain other noncommercial uses permitted by copyright law.

This book is a work of fiction. Names, characters, places, and incidents are products of the author's imagination or are used fictitiously. Any resemblance to actual events, locales, or persons, living or dead, is entirely coincidental.

ISBN: 978-969-36-9282-2 E-book
ISBN: 978-969-36-9283-9 Paperback
ISBN: 978-969-36-9284-6 Hardcover

Published by |

Table of Contents

Introduction 1

    Purpose of the Book 3

    The Power of Quotes in Business 6

Chapter 1 Leadership & Vision 9

    What Makes a Leader? 13

    Visionary Quotes: Lighting the Path of Progress and Inspiration 16

    Applying Vision in Business Decisions 20

Chapter 2 Teamwork & Collaboration 24

    The Strength of Unity 27

    Team-Building Quotes: Harnessing the Wisdom for Collective Growth 30

    The Value of Diverse Perspectives 34

Chapter 3 Innovation & Creativity 38

    Pioneering the Future 41

    Inspirational Quotes on Innovation 45

    Encouraging Creativity in the Workplace 49

Chapter 4 Decision Making & Strategy 54

    Navigating Business Choices 58

    Strategic Quotes for Success 64

The Role of Intuition in Business 68

Chapter 5 Ethics & Integrity **74**

The Backbone of Trust 79

Timeless Quotes on Integrity 83

Building and Maintaining Trust in Business 88

Chapter 6 Resilience & Overcoming Challenges **94**

Embracing Setbacks as Learning Opportunities 99

Motivational Quotes for Tough Times 103

Case Studies of Resilience in Business 108

Chapter 7 Communication & Influence **114**

The Art of Effective Communication 119

Powerful Quotes on Influence 124

Crafting Messages That Resonate 128

Chapter 8 Growth & Continuous Learning **133**

The Journey of Self-Improvement 137

Quotes on the Importance of Learning: A Deep Dive into Lifelong Education 142

Strategies for Personal and Professional Growth 147

Chapter 9 Work-Life Balance & Self-Care **152**

Nurturing the Self in a Busy World 157

Quotes on Balance and Well-being 161

Practical Tips for Maintaining Balance 165

Chapter 10 Legacy & Impact **171**

Beyond the Bottom Line:Rethinking Business Success 175

Inspiring Quotes on Legacy:More than Footprints in the Sands of Time .. 179

Making a Lasting Difference in Business and Beyond 183

Conclusion The Harmonious Intersection of Business and Impact 187

Reflecting on the Journey:A Tapestry of Insights, Aspirations, and Transformations 190

The Future of Business Success:A Blend of Innovation, Ethics, and Human-Centric Approaches 193

Introduction

Purpose of the Book

In every corridor of the business world, from the bustling floors of start-ups to the pristine offices of multinational corporations, there's an underlying force that drives individuals and teams toward success. It's not always about strategies, marketing plans, or financial forecasts. Sometimes, it's about inspiration—the kind that comes from a few carefully chosen words that resonate with our experiences, aspirations, and visions.

"In the Boardroom & Beyond: Quotes to Drive Business Success" is a collection and exploration of these words, but it's more than just a compilation. This book dives deep into the essence of each quote, unraveling its relevance in the business realm and revealing its power to inspire, motivate, and guide.

The Power of Quotes in Business

But why quotes? In the digital age, with information at our fingertips, why do simple, concise strings of words still hold power?

Universality

A good quote transcends its origin. Whether it comes from a tech mogul, a historical general, or a philosopher from an era long gone, its message remains relevant, striking chords across time and industries.

Simplicity

In the business world, where jargon can often obfuscate meaning, the simplicity of a quote cuts through the noise. It delivers wisdom in a digestible format, easy to remember and repeat.

Emotional Resonance: Quotes often encapsulate profound emotions—hope, ambition, fear, resilience. They remind us that behind every business decision or strategy lies a human element, an emotional core.

Guidance and Reflection

Especially in times of uncertainty or challenge, quotes act as lighthouses, guiding us through rough waters, offering a moment of introspection and recalibration.

The Structure and Journey Ahead

As we navigate through this book, each chapter addresses a fundamental area of business, from leadership and innovation to ethics and legacy. Within these chapters, quotes are not merely listed but are dissected, explored, and contextualized. They become launching pads for deeper discussions, for stories of success and lessons from failures, for strategies and actionable insights.

Moreover, this book acknowledges the changing face of the modern business landscape. As we stand on the brink of technological revolutions, amidst societal shifts and a renewed emphasis on sustainability and ethics, these quotes are more than reflections of the past. They are roadmaps for the future, highlighting timeless principles that can guide businesses in an ever-evolving world.

Lastly, this isn't a book meant to be consumed passively. It's a tool, a companion. As you read, reflect on your journey, your challenges, and your vision. Let these quotes be mirrors, revealing facets of your business self, or windows, opening vistas of what you can achieve.

In Conclusion

"In the Boardroom & Beyond" is a tribute to the power of words and the indomitable spirit of business. It's a recognition of the paths tread by those before us and an invitation to forge our paths. As we delve into this exploration, may you find wisdom, inspiration, and above all, a renewed zeal to drive towards unparalleled business success.

This introduction sets the tone for the chapters that follow, emphasizing the significance of quotes in the business realm and highlighting the journey the reader is about to embark on.

Purpose of the Book

As the great playwright George Bernard Shaw once wrote, "The single biggest problem in communication is the illusion that it has taken place." Throughout history, thinkers, leaders, and innovators have grappled with the challenge of articulating ideas, inspiring teams, and driving change. This struggle is no more evident than in the world of business, where competition, evolution, and innovation are daily realities. The purpose of "In the Boardroom & Beyond: Quotes to Drive Business Success" is to bridge the gap between mere communication and profound understanding, offering readers a curated tapestry of insights woven from the most impactful quotes relevant to the business world.

The Essence of a Quote

At its core, a quote is the distillation of a complex idea into its most essential and poignant form. It captures the zeitgeist of a moment or the wisdom of an era, crystallizing it in a way that resonates universally. This book's aim is not to provide a mere catalog of quotes but to dive into their essence, revealing the deeper currents of wisdom they contain and their applicability in the modern business landscape.

Beyond the Boardroom

Why extend our exploration beyond the boardroom? Business is more than the sum of its monetary transactions and strategic decisions. It's a human enterprise, filled with aspirations, challenges, breakthroughs, and disappointments. The "beyond" in the book's title signifies this expansive view of business – touching upon life lessons, ethical dilemmas, leadership challenges, and the continuous journey of personal growth and self-discovery.

Guidance for the Modern Entrepreneur and Leader

As the global business environment becomes more interconnected, volatile, and complex, there is a dire need for guidance – markers that help leaders and entrepreneurs navigate their journey. The carefully chosen quotes and accompanying discussions in this book serve as these markers. They offer guidance and, more importantly, a reflective space for leaders to recalibrate their compasses, ensuring they're not only effective in their roles but also aligned with their deeper purpose and values.

A Journey Through Time and Wisdom

Another purpose of this book is to take readers on a temporal journey. The quotes span various eras, cultures, and disciplines, providing a multi-faceted view of business wisdom. By understanding the context of each quote and its relevance today, readers gain a panoramic view of business evolution, with lessons from the past illuminating paths for the future.

Quotes as Catalysts for Change

In the rapidly evolving business landscape, adaptability and innovation are key. The insights encapsulated in these quotes act as catalysts, challenging preconceived notions and urging readers to think differently. They inspire change, not just in strategies and operations but in mindsets – the very way we approach business challenges.

A Repository for All

One of the primary purposes of this collection is its universal appeal. Whether you're a seasoned CEO, a budding entrepreneur, a mid-level manager, or someone just entering the business world, there's something in this book for you. It's designed to be both a quick reference guide for moments when you need immediate inspiration and a comprehensive manual for deeper contemplation.

Building a Legacy with Words

Finally, this book is about legacy. In business, leaders are often remembered for their decisions, their innovations, and their success metrics. But beyond that, they're remembered for their words – the ideas they championed, the visions they painted, and the values they upheld. By engaging deeply with the quotes in this book, readers are not just absorbing wisdom but are also being equipped to articulate and build their legacy, one profound insight at a time.

In Conclusion

The purpose of "In the Boardroom & Beyond" is manifold. It seeks to inspire, guide, challenge, and support. It aims to be a beacon for those navigating the tumultuous seas of business and a comforting fire for those seeking reflection. In its pages lies not just the wisdom of ages but the promise of a future where business success is as much about profound insights as it is about profits. As you delve deeper into this book, may each quote be a stepping stone, leading you to the zenith of your business journey.

This detailed explanation of the book's purpose offers readers a clear roadmap of what to expect and underscores the profound impact that words, particularly in the form of quotes, can have in the realm of business and personal growth.

The Power of Quotes in Business

The tapestry of the business world, with its intricate patterns of decision-making, strategies, and human interactions, is colored by countless influences. Among them, quotes stand out as small, potent threads that can subtly shape and redefine its texture. But what makes these brief, often simple strings of words so influential in a domain defined by hard facts, figures, and analytics? To comprehend the full magnitude of the power of quotes in business, we must embark on a journey that delves into the psyche of businesses, their leaders, and the very fabric of organizational culture.

Distilling Wisdom into Words

At their core, quotes are the quintessence of wisdom, knowledge, or insight condensed into a compact form. The business realm, with its continuous cycle of challenges and triumphs, requires consistent sources of inspiration and reflection. A well-chosen quote can encapsulate the learnings from an entire lifetime or the essence of a complex strategy. In this succinctness lies potency; a quote provides a bite-sized nugget of wisdom, making it accessible and easy to remember in the fast-paced business environment.

Emotional Resonance: The Human Side of Business

Beyond the balance sheets, growth charts, and strategy meetings, businesses thrive on the human spirit. Emotions, aspirations, fears, and motivations are the underlying currents of every organization. Quotes have an uncanny ability to resonate on an emotional level. They act as mirrors, reflecting our innermost thoughts and feelings, or windows, offering a glimpse into uncharted territories of understanding. In doing so, they tap into the core of what makes businesses truly thrive – the people.

Bridging the Past, Present, and Future

A well-curated quote carries with it the weight of history. Whether it's a piece of advice from a business magnate of yesteryears or a visionary prediction from decades ago that holds true today, quotes bridge the temporal gap. They bring lessons from the past, offer reflections for the present, and provide guidance for the future. This temporal bridging ensures that businesses don't operate in a vacuum but are constantly informed by the accumulated wisdom of ages.

Instigating Reflection and Critical Thinking

In the hustle and bustle of daily operations, it's easy for individuals and businesses to get caught in a reactive mode. A thought-provoking quote can serve as a pause button, compelling leaders and teams to step back and reflect. By challenging prevailing thoughts or presenting a fresh perspective, quotes can instigate critical thinking, leading to more informed decisions and innovative solutions.

An Anchor in the Storm

The world of business is fraught with uncertainties. Economic downturns, market disruptions, or unforeseen challenges can leave even the most seasoned professionals feeling adrift. In such times, a powerful quote can act as an anchor, offering stability and reassurance. It can remind leaders and teams of fundamental truths, helping them navigate challenges with resilience and tenacity.

Facilitating Communication and Alignment

A shared quote can become a rallying cry, a mission statement, or a common point of reference within an organization. When teams or entire organizations align behind the essence of a quote, it facilitates communication and fosters a sense of shared purpose. The quote becomes more than words; it evolves into a symbol of collective values and vision.

Elevating Brand Identity and Legacy

Many successful brands have harnessed the power of quotes to elevate their identity. Whether it's a tagline that resonates with audiences or a guiding principle that shapes company culture, the right quote can become synonymous with a brand's legacy. It's a testament to how words, when chosen and employed effectively, can shape perception, influence behavior, and drive brand loyalty.

In Conclusion

In the expansive universe of business, quotes are like stars – small, luminous points that can guide, inspire, and enlighten. Their power lies not just in the words themselves but in their ability to transcend them, touching upon universal truths and human experiences. As businesses evolve, grow, and face new frontiers of challenges and opportunities, quotes will remain steadfast companions, illuminating the path with the combined wisdom of ages. In their brevity, they capture the vastness of experience, ensuring that businesses don't just operate but thrive with insight, purpose, and a deep connection to the human spirit.

Chapter 1
Leadership & Vision

In the annals of business, one theme persistently stands out as the bedrock upon which empires are built and legacies are cemented: leadership. Leadership, however, is not a monolithic concept. It's multifaceted, evolving, and, above all, rooted in vision. This chapter seeks to explore the symbiotic relationship between leadership and vision, unraveled through poignant quotes that have illuminated this intricate dance over the years.

The Essence of Leadership

To truly understand leadership, one must first dispel the notion that it's synonymous with authority. Leadership isn't about titles or hierarchical positions; it's an embodiment of influence, impact, and inspiration. As John C. Maxwell aptly put it, "Leadership is not about titles, positions, or flowcharts. It is about one life influencing another." This encapsulates the essence of leadership: the power to shape, guide, and influence thoughts, actions, and outcomes.

The Role of Vision in Leadership

At the heart of impactful leadership lies vision. Vision is the North Star, the guiding light that provides direction and purpose. It's the blueprint of a future yet to be built. As Joel A. Barker quipped, "Vision without action is merely a dream. Action without vision just passes the time. Vision with action can change the world." This underscores the imperative for leaders to not only possess a vision but to actively work towards it, turning abstract dreams into tangible realities.

Symbiosis: Where Leadership and Vision Intersect

Leadership and vision are inextricably linked, with each amplifying the other's power. A leader without a vision is like a ship without a compass, aimlessly adrift. Conversely, a vision without effective leadership remains an ephemeral dream, lacking direction and execution. When these two forces merge, they create a dynamic synergy, propelling businesses forward with momentum and purpose.

The Evolution of Leadership

Historically, leadership in business was often equated with autocracy – a top-down approach where decisions were dictated and employees followed orders. However, as Robert K. Greenleaf aptly noted in coining the term "servant leadership": "The servant-leader is servant first... It begins with the natural feeling that one wants to serve, to serve first." Modern leadership paradigms emphasize collaboration, empathy, and empowerment. They recognize that the best leaders serve their teams, fostering environments where every member feels valued, heard, and motivated.

Challenges in Visionary Leadership

While the marriage of leadership and vision sounds idyllic, it's not without challenges. Crafting a compelling vision requires foresight, insight, and intuition. Yet, as Bill Gates observed, "We always overestimate the change that will occur in the next two years and underestimate the change that will occur in the next ten." Visionary leadership demands a delicate balance between pragmatism and ambition, between immediate realities and future possibilities.

Cultivating Vision

A common misconception is that vision is the exclusive domain of the chosen few – the rare geniuses blessed with prophetic insights. Yet, as Peter Drucker pointed out, "The best way to predict the future is to create it." Vision is as much about creativity as it is about foresight. Leaders can cultivate vision by constantly learning, staying attuned to market trends, understanding customer needs, and most importantly, daring to dream and think outside the box.

Leading with Authenticity

In the pursuit of vision, leaders must remain true to themselves and their values. Authenticity is the cornerstone of trust, and without trust, even the most grandiose visions remain unrealized. As Oprah Winfrey, a paragon of authentic leadership, stated, "Real integrity is doing the right thing, knowing that nobody's going to know whether you did it or not." For leaders, walking the talk and leading with authenticity ensures that their vision is embraced and championed by those they lead.

The Legacy of Visionary Leaders

Leaders come and go, but their legacies endure, immortalized in the visions they championed and the changes they effected. As Steve Jobs, one of the most iconic visionary leaders, reflected, "Being the richest man in the cemetery doesn't matter to me. Going to bed at night saying we've done something wonderful... that's what matters to me." Visionary leaders are remembered not for their accolades or achievements but for the transformative impact of their visions.

In Conclusion

Leadership, in its truest form, is a dance with vision. It's a journey that weaves through the annals of history, through successes and failures, aspirations, and realizations. The quotes peppered throughout this chapter are more than words; they're signposts, marking the milestones of this intricate journey. They remind us that leadership, at its heart, is a quest for a better tomorrow. And vision is the compass that ensures we're headed in the right direction. As we move forward in the business world, may we all harness the power of visionary leadership, shaping futures, and leaving indelible legacies.

What Makes a Leader?

The leadership landscape is as vast and varied as the personalities that occupy its realm. What makes someone a leader? Is it their ability to inspire? Their vision? Or perhaps their ability to influence and guide? In this exploration, we'll delve deep into the various facets that truly define a leader, drawing upon historical examples, psychological insights, and the wisdom of time-tested philosophies.

Defining Leadership: More Than a Title

It's imperative to begin by dispelling the myth that leadership is synonymous with a position or title. While leaders can occupy positions of authority, true leadership transcends hierarchies. It's about influence, impact, and inspiration. As Dwight D. Eisenhower once said, "Leadership is the art of getting someone else to do something you want done because he wants to do it." Leadership, therefore, is as much about the heart as it is about the head.

Vision: The North Star

Every great leader is guided by a compelling vision—a clear mental image of what could be, driven by the conviction that it should be. Vision acts as the North Star, providing direction and purpose. Without vision, leadership becomes aimless. A leader's vision embodies hope and paves the way for the future, challenging the status quo and daring to imagine a world different from the present.

Emotional Intelligence (EQ): The Heart of Leadership

In his groundbreaking work on emotional intelligence, Daniel Goleman posited that EQ might matter more than IQ for leaders. The five components of EQ—self-awareness, self-regulation, motivation, empathy, and social skills—play crucial roles in leadership. Leaders with high EQ are attuned to their emotions and those of others, facilitating better teamwork, decision-making, and conflict resolution.

Resilience and Adaptability

The road to realizing a vision is seldom smooth. Leaders face obstacles, setbacks, and failures. What distinguishes them is their resilience—the ability to bounce back, learn from setbacks, and forge ahead with renewed determination. Coupled with resilience is adaptability: the capability to adjust strategies and tactics while staying true to the overarching vision.

Integrity:Leadership's Moral Compass

Leadership without integrity is like a ship without a compass—it may move but will likely drift off course. Integrity is the congruence between words and actions. Leaders with integrity are trustworthy, honest, and consistent, making them reliable anchors for their teams and organizations.

Empowering Others

Leadership is not about hoarding power but dispersing it. Great leaders empower others, creating an environment where team members feel valued, capable, and trusted. By delegating responsibilities and entrusting tasks, leaders not only build capacity but also foster growth and self-efficacy among team members.

Continuous Learning and Growth

The best leaders recognize that leadership is a journey, not a destination. They are perpetual students, always seeking to expand their knowledge, refine their skills, and evolve with the changing dynamics of the world around them. This growth mindset ensures they remain relevant, effective, and inspiring.

Effective Communication

The ability to communicate effectively is a linchpin of great leadership. Leaders must convey complex ideas, motivate with persuasive messages, and listen actively. Effective communication bridges the gap between a leader's vision and the team's understanding, ensuring alignment and collective movement towards goals.

Building Relationships and Fostering Collaboration

No leader operates in isolation. Building strong relationships based on trust, respect, and mutual understanding is foundational to leadership success. By fostering collaboration, leaders leverage the collective intelligence, skills, and efforts of the team, leading to enhanced creativity and productivity.

Legacy and Impact

True leaders think beyond their tenure, focusing on the long-term impact and legacy they leave behind. They invest in future leaders, nurture sustainable practices, and build enduring institutions. Their influence persists long after their direct involvement, embedded in the cultures they've shaped and the lives they've touched.

In Conclusion

Leadership is an intricate tapestry woven from threads of character, skills, and experiences. It's an amalgamation of the mind's clarity, the heart's passion, and the soul's purpose. While certain traits and skills can enhance leadership potential, the essence of leadership is deeply personal and continually evolving.

The world has witnessed various leadership styles—from transformational and servant leadership to autocratic and laissez-faire approaches. Yet, regardless of style or method, the true measure of a leader lies in their ability to inspire positive change, to uplift those around them, and to chart a course towards a brighter future. In the end, leadership is not just about being in charge; it's about taking care of those in one's charge, weaving a narrative of hope, progress, and shared success.

Visionary Quotes:Lighting the Path of Progress and Inspiration

Quotes have an innate power. With just a few words, they can encapsulate vast ideas, evoke profound emotions, and inspire monumental change. Visionary quotes, in particular, transcend the limitations of time and context, speaking to universal aspirations and dreams. These quotes reflect not just fleeting thoughts but foundational philosophies that shape worlds. Let's dive deep into some of the most profound visionary quotes, exploring their depths and the luminaries behind them.

"The only thing worse than being blind is having sight but no vision."

– *Helen Keller*

Helen Keller, despite her early-life challenges with blindness and deafness, emerged as a staunch advocate for the disabled and an inspirational figure for many. This quote underscores the distinction between mere physical sight and inner vision—a deeper, more profound understanding and foresight. It reminds us that the most significant disability can be a lack of perspective and purpose.

"If you want to build a ship, don't drum up people to collect wood and don't assign them tasks and work, but rather teach them to long for the endless immensity of the sea."

– *Antoine de Saint-Exupéry*

Saint-Exupéry, a pioneering French aviator and the author of 'The Little Prince,' captures the essence of inspiration in leadership. Instead of dictating tasks, a visionary leader instills a passion and a purpose. They make others see the larger picture, the grand vision, thereby fostering intrinsic motivation.

"Your time is limited, don't waste it living someone else's life."

– *Steve Jobs*

Jobs, the co-founder of Apple, was known for his relentless pursuit of innovation. This quote encapsulates the philosophy of living authentically. It underscores the value of individuality and the importance of pursuing one's vision and passion, unfettered by societal expectations or conventions.

"The future belongs to those who believe in the beauty of their dreams."

– *Eleanor Roosevelt*

A First Lady, diplomat, and activist, Eleanor Roosevelt firmly believed in the power of dreams and vision. Her words remind us that the future isn't a predetermined fate but a canvas awaiting the strokes of dreamers. It emphasizes the transformative power of belief and the potential it holds.

"Vision without action is merely a dream. Action without vision just passes the time. Vision with action can change the world."

– *Joel A. Barker*

Barker, a scholar and author, emphasizes the symbiotic relationship between vision and action. While vision charts the course, action propels forward movement. Together, they have the power to bring about lasting change, reminding us that dreaming is just the beginning; it's the execution that brings dreams to life.

"To foresee the future, one must first understand the past."

– *Confucius*

The ancient Chinese philosopher, Confucius, highlights the importance of historical perspective in shaping the future. True visionaries aren't just forward-thinkers; they are students of history, understanding patterns, lessons, and insights from the past to inform and guide their future endeavors.

"The empires of the future are the empires of the mind."

– *Winston Churchill*

Churchill, the wartime Prime Minister of the UK, foresaw a time when physical might would be secondary to intellectual prowess and vision. In our current age of technology, innovation, and information, his prediction seems ever more prescient. Visionaries today aren't just conquerors; they are thinkers, innovators, and dreamers.

"Dream no small dreams for they have no power to move the hearts of men."

– Johann Wolfgang von Goethe

The German writer and statesman, Goethe, underscores the magnitude of dreams. Visionaries don't settle for mediocrity; they dream big, aiming to inspire, challenge, and transform. It's the grandeur of their vision that captivates and mobilizes.

"Create with the heart; build with the mind."

– Criss Jami

Poet and essayist Criss Jami captures the duality of vision. While the heart's passion and emotion birth visions, it's the strategic, analytical mind that turns these visions into realities. Visionaries master this delicate dance between emotion and intellect.

"The best way to predict the future is to create it."

– Peter Drucker

Management guru Peter Drucker's words serve as a clarion call for proactive action. Visionaries don't just passively predict the future; they actively mold and shape it. They are architects of destiny, not mere bystanders.

In Conclusion

Visionary quotes are more than just words on paper; they are philosophies that drive action, influence thought, and shape societies. These nuggets of wisdom serve as lighthouses, guiding us through tumultuous seas, reminding us of our purpose, and illuminating our paths. They come from varied sources—poets, leaders, philosophers, innovators—but they converge on universal truths about vision, dreams, and the indomitable human spirit.

In the ever-evolving tapestry of human history, visionary quotes stand out as threads of gold, weaving patterns of hope, ambition, and inspiration. As we navigate the complexities of our times, may these words serve as beacons, reminding us of the transformative power of vision and the endless possibilities it heralds.

Applying Vision in Business Decisions

In the bustling realm of business, where decisions are made at the speed of light and stakes are high, a clear and compelling vision can be the compass that provides direction and purpose. Vision, in this context, isn't a fleeting dream but a guiding philosophy that influences every facet of the business, from strategic planning to daily operations. Let's delve into the nuances of applying vision in business decisions, exploring its significance, methodology, and transformative potential.

The Essence of Vision in Business

Vision in business encapsulates an organization's aspirations, defining its purpose beyond mere profit-making. It provides an answer to the quintessential question: "Why do we exist?" This vision becomes the North Star, guiding the ship of business through turbulent waters and ensuring alignment in strategy and action.

The Alignment of Strategy with Vision

Strategic decisions, be it market expansion, product diversification, or mergers and acquisitions, must be rooted in the company's vision. When a strategy aligns with vision, it resonates with the organization's core values and principles. For instance, if a company's vision emphasizes sustainability, then its strategies should prioritize eco-friendly practices and green innovation.

Vision and Organizational Culture

The decisions surrounding organizational culture—values, norms, behaviors—should mirror the company's vision. If the vision is about innovation, then fostering a culture that encourages experimentation, celebrates failures as learning opportunities, and provides platforms for idea generation becomes vital.

Talent Management and Vision

Decisions about hiring, training, and development should be influenced by the company's vision. Organizations should seek individuals who not only possess the requisite skills but also resonate with the company's vision. Training and development programs should be designed to imbue employees with the vision, ensuring they become its ambassadors.

Product Development and Visionary Insights

When a company's vision is centered on addressing specific societal needs or challenges, product development decisions should be geared towards solutions that echo this vision. For instance, a vision centered on enhancing global health should influence decisions to develop products that address critical health challenges or improve wellness.

Financial Decisions Through the Lens of Vision

While profitability is a primary concern, financial decisions—like investments, budget allocations, and funding—should also be vetted against the company's vision. Investing in ventures or initiatives that contradict the vision can erode stakeholder trust and dilute brand value.

Marketing and Branding: Amplifying Vision

Marketing and branding decisions offer a platform to communicate the company's vision to the world. From advertising campaigns to CSR initiatives, every decision should amplify the vision, ensuring it resonates with consumers and differentiates the brand in the marketplace.

Navigating Crises with Vision

In times of crises, be it financial downturns, public relations debacles, or global disruptions like pandemics, a company's vision can be its anchor. Decisions made during these times, if aligned with the vision, can bolster stakeholder confidence and pave the way for recovery and resurgence.

Long-term Planning: Vision as the Blueprint

While short-term gains are essential, visionary companies are defined by their long-term thinking. Decisions about future growth, expansions, and innovations should be mapped out keeping the vision in mind, ensuring sustainability and relevance in the ever-evolving business landscape.

Feedback and Evolution: Keeping the Vision Relevant

The business world isn't static. As market dynamics, technological advancements, and societal needs evolve, companies should periodically revisit their vision. Decisions about refining and adapting the vision based on feedback from stakeholders and changing scenarios ensure that the vision remains relevant and potent.

In Conclusion

Applying vision in business decisions isn't a mere idealistic endeavor; it's a strategic imperative. Vision breathes life into strategies, fortifies the company's brand, galvanizes its workforce, and fosters trust among stakeholders. It ensures coherence in action, alignment in intent, and authenticity in approach.

However, merely crafting a grand vision isn't sufficient. Its true power is unlocked when it's deeply ingrained in the company's DNA, influencing decisions at every level, from the boardroom to the shop floor. In a world marked by volatilities and uncertainties, a well-articulated and diligently applied vision can be the beacon that lights the path towards sustainable success, societal impact, and legacy creation. As businesses continue to navigate the complexities of the 21st century, may vision be their guiding light, illuminating the path of purpose, progress, and prosperity.

Chapter 2
Teamwork & Collaboration

In the symphony of business, every role is pivotal. Like instruments in an orchestra, when teams come together in harmony, they create a melody that's greater than the sum of its parts. Teamwork and collaboration aren't just buzzwords; they're the lifeblood of successful businesses. In this chapter, we'll explore the nuances, challenges, and rewards of fostering a culture rooted in collaboration.

Defining Teamwork & Collaboration

Teamwork is the collective effort of a group to achieve a shared goal or complete a task, while collaboration involves the sharing of ideas, skills, and expertise. Collaboration is the heart of teamwork; it's where individual talents and insights fuse to birth innovative solutions and drive collective progress.

The Evolution of Teamwork in Business

From assembly lines in the industrial age to cross-functional teams in the digital era, teamwork has continuously evolved. Today, with globalization and digitalization, teams often span continents, cultures, and time zones, making collaboration both a challenge and a necessity.

The Symbiotic Relationship between Leadership and Team Dynamics

The efficacy of a team isn't solely contingent on its members but also on its leadership. A leader's role is to guide, inspire, and create an environment where collaboration thrives. They act as the maestro, ensuring each team member feels valued, understood, and aligned with the collective goal.

The Power of Diverse Teams

Diversity isn't merely a box to tick; it's a business imperative. Diverse teams bring varied perspectives, experiences, and problem-solving approaches. This richness can lead to more innovative solutions, wider market understanding, and better decision-making.

Overcoming Collaboration Challenges

While collaboration has immense benefits, it's not devoid of challenges—conflicting views, cultural differences, communication barriers, and more. Successful teams acknowledge these challenges and employ strategies like open communication, conflict resolution mechanisms, and regular feedback loops to mitigate them.

Tools and Technologies Facilitating Collaboration

The digital age has ushered in a plethora of tools designed to bolster collaboration. Platforms like Slack, Microsoft Teams, and Trello have made real-time communication, project tracking, and resource sharing more streamlined than ever, ensuring that even remote teams can work in harmony.

The Psychological Dynamics of Teamwork

Humans, by nature, are social beings. The psychological aspects of teamwork, like the sense of belonging, shared purpose, and mutual respect, can boost morale, job satisfaction, and even personal growth. Conversely, a dysfunctional team can lead to stress, dissatisfaction, and burnout.

Collaboration Beyond Borders: The Global Team

Today's businesses often operate on a global scale. This global footprint means collaborating across borders, cultures, and time zones. Embracing cultural nuances, understanding local market dynamics, and fostering a culture of inclusivity are pivotal in harnessing the full potential of global teams.

Measuring the Impact of Teamwork and Collaboration

The outcomes of effective teamwork are manifold—enhanced productivity, improved problem-solving, increased innovation, and boosted morale. Employing metrics and KPIs to gauge teamwork effectiveness, such as project delivery times, team satisfaction scores, or innovative solutions generated, can help organizations continuously refine their collaboration strategies.

Future Trends: The Evolving Landscape of Teamwork and Collaboration

With the rise of AI, remote work, and a shift towards gig-based economies, the future of teamwork and collaboration is set for a sea change. Embracing these shifts, preparing for new collaboration paradigms, and fostering a culture of adaptability will be key for businesses to thrive in the coming decades.

In Conclusion

Teamwork and collaboration are more than mere aspects of organizational operations; they are the very foundations upon which businesses are built. As organizations grow and evolve, so do their teams. The magic lies in harnessing the collective prowess of these teams, fostering a culture where individual talents are celebrated, and collaborative efforts are championed.

In a world that's increasingly interconnected and interdependent, the ability to collaborate effectively—both within and outside organizational boundaries—will be a defining factor for business success. As businesses stride forward into the future, may they remember the age-old adage: "Together, we achieve more." With collaboration at their core, businesses can not only achieve their goals but set new benchmarks, pioneering pathways of innovation, growth, and sustainable success.

The Strength of Unity

The ancient storytellers and wise men spoke of it, the modern leaders and thinkers advocate for it – unity, a force that has been, time and again, emphasized as the linchpin of strength. From families to organizations, nations to global alliances, the strength of unity binds individuals together, propelling them towards shared aspirations and victories. But what makes unity so powerful? Let's dive deep into this concept, deciphering its essence, manifestations, challenges, and its undeniable impact.

Unity Defined: More than Just Togetherness

While the essence of unity revolves around coming together, it transcends mere physical or superficial aggregation. Unity is a harmonious blend of thoughts, purposes, and efforts, where individual identities, while preserved, contribute to a larger collective goal.

Historical Implications of Unity

History brims with tales where unity played a pivotal role. Whether it was tribes uniting to form formidable kingdoms, nations joining hands during world wars, or civil rights activists rallying collectively for justice, the strength of unity has shaped epochs.

Psychological Roots: The Innate Human Need

Humans, being inherently social creatures, have always sought connection. The power of unity satiates this inherent need for belongingness and connection, providing a sense of purpose, security, and shared destiny.

Unity in Diversity: A Tapestry of Colors and Threads

One of the most profound manifestations of unity is the celebration of diversity. It's not about being identical but about harmonizing differences. Like an orchestra producing a symphony from varied instruments, unity thrives in diversity, drawing strength from individual peculiarities and contributions.

The Economic and Social Implications of Unity

Nations and economies benefit immensely from unity. Unified economic policies, collaborative scientific ventures, or joint cultural events can lead to exponential growth, shared resources, and synergistic outcomes. Conversely, disunity can lead to stagnation, conflicts, and societal rifts.

Challenges to Unity: The Divisive Forces

In a world teeming with diverse ideologies, interests, and ambitions, unity often faces threats. From political divides, cultural misunderstandings, to economic disparities, these divisive forces often challenge the strength and fabric of unity.

Fostering Unity: The Role of Leaders and Institutions

Leaders, be it in families, organizations, or nations, play a cardinal role in fostering unity. Through inclusive policies, empathetic communication, and actions that prioritize collective good, they can galvanize individuals, bridging divides and nurturing unity.

Unity and Innovation: The Creative Powerhouse

When minds unite, innovation thrives. Diverse perspectives, when unified towards a shared objective, lead to creative problem-solving, novel ideas, and groundbreaking innovations. From technological marvels to artistic masterpieces, unity often lies at the heart of creation.

Unity in Modern Times: The Digital & Global Era

In an age where digital platforms connect individuals globally, the potential for unity is unparalleled. Movements like climate change activism or global health initiatives showcase the strength of global unity, where borders dissolve and humanity unites for shared causes.

The Future of Unity: Evolving Concepts and Challenges

As the world becomes more interconnected, the dynamics of unity too will evolve. Will technological advancements strengthen or dilute unity? How will socio-political changes mold the concept of unity in the future? While the answers are yet to unfold, one thing remains certain – the undying relevance of unity.

In Conclusion

The strength of unity is an age-old concept, resonating across cultures, eras, and realms. While it is often lauded in philosophical discourses or poetic renditions, its real power is palpable in tangible outcomes – from successful enterprises, peaceful societies to evolved civilizations.

The potency of unity lies in its ability to harness individual strengths, mitigate weaknesses, and foster a sense of collective purpose. Like the age-old adage goes, "A single twig breaks, but a bundle of twigs is strong." As we navigate the complexities of the modern world, may we continually recognize, celebrate, and leverage the unparalleled strength of unity. In unity, we find resilience, progress, and a beacon of hope, illuminating paths of collective triumphs and sustainable futures.

Team-Building Quotes: Harnessing the Wisdom for Collective Growth

Quotes, succinct yet profound, encapsulate wisdom that otherwise demands volumes. Team-building quotes, in particular, serve as micro lessons, illuminating the essence of collaboration, unity, and shared aspirations. Let's delve deep into some of the most impactful team-building quotes and unravel the wisdom each one beholds.

"Alone we can do so little; together we can do so much."

— Helen Keller

Helen Keller, despite her challenges, recognized the power of unity. This quote emphasizes that while individual effort is potent, collective action amplifies outcomes. In the world of business, sports, or any collective venture, this holds unequivocally true. When diverse skills and strengths are unified, they overcome individual limitations, making achievements boundless.

"Talent wins games, but teamwork and intelligence win championships."

— Michael Jordan

Jordan, a basketball legend, encapsulates a universal truth. Talent might give a temporary edge, but sustainable success, the kind that writes history, comes from teamwork. Teamwork, combined with strategic thinking, can overcome even the most formidable opponents. In organizational contexts, it reminds leaders to prioritize collective effort over individual brilliance for long-term success.

"Coming together is a beginning. Keeping together is progress. Working together is success."

— Henry Ford

Ford's words chronicle the journey of teamwork. Merely forming a team is just the inception. The real challenge lies in nurturing cohesion and facilitating collaborative endeavors. This quote is a reminder that teamwork is a continuous journey, demanding patience, understanding, and collective drive.

"Unity is strength... when there is teamwork and collaboration, wonderful things can be achieved."

– Mattie Stepanek

Stepanek, a young poet with wisdom beyond his years, emphasizes the magic of collaboration. This quote underscores that unity doesn't just magnify strength but transforms it. In realms like business, social ventures, or community projects, collaboration can yield results that were once deemed unattainable.

"The strength of the team is each individual member. The strength of each member is the team."

– Phil Jackson

Jackson, with his coaching acumen, highlights the symbiotic relationship between a team and its members. It signifies that a team's prowess is the sum total of its individual strengths. Conversely, an individual's success is also anchored in the team's support, resources, and collective wisdom.

"None of us is as smart as all of us."

– Ken Blanchard

Blanchard's quote is a humbling reminder of collective intelligence. Even the brightest mind can't match the diverse perspectives, experiences, and problem-solving capabilities of a collective. Organizations can leverage this by fostering open dialogues, brainstorming sessions, and inclusive decision-making processes.

"Great things in business are never done by one person; they're done by a team of people."

– Steve Jobs

Steve Jobs, known for his visionary leadership at Apple, recognized the essence of teamwork in business success. This quote emphasizes that monumental achievements, be they groundbreaking products or revolutionary services, are the fruits of collective labor, passion, and innovation.

"If everyone is moving forward together, then success takes care of itself."

– Abraham Lincoln

Lincoln, with his leadership during tumultuous times, knew the essence of unified progression. This quote is a reminder that success is a natural outcome when efforts are synchronized and directed towards a shared goal.

"Teamwork begins by building trust. And the only way to do that is to overcome our need for invulnerability."

– Patrick Lencioni

Lencioni, in his quote, touches upon a crucial aspect of teamwork – vulnerability. Authentic collaboration requires trust, which stems from openness, transparency, and the courage to be vulnerable. It reminds leaders and team members to shed their guards, embrace authenticity, and foster a culture of mutual trust.

"The best teamwork comes from men who are working independently toward one goal in unison."

– James Cash Penney

Penney's insight stresses the importance of individual autonomy within a team framework. For a team to thrive, members should be empowered to work independently while staying aligned with the collective vision. It signifies a balance between autonomy and collaboration.

In Conclusion

Team-building quotes, with their brevity, capture the essence of collective endeavors. They serve as reminders, lessons, and inspirations, echoing the undeniable truth that in unity lies strength. As teams navigate challenges, face adversities, or celebrate triumphs, these quotes can act as guiding beacons, illuminating the path of collaboration, trust, and shared aspirations.

Harnessing the wisdom from these quotes, organizations, leaders, and individuals can foster environments where teamwork is not just practiced but revered. After all, in the harmonious symphony of collaboration, lies the melody of unparalleled success and growth.

The Value of Diverse Perspectives

In an ever-evolving world, where globalization has brought different cultures and communities into closer proximity, the value of diverse perspectives cannot be overstated. These varied viewpoints, borne from different backgrounds, experiences, and understandings, enrich discussions, drive innovation, and foster holistic growth. By delving deep into the significance of diverse perspectives, we can better appreciate their transformative power.

The Multifaceted Gem of Diversity

Every individual, shaped by unique life experiences, cultures, upbringing, and intrinsic factors, carries a unique lens of perception. Just as every facet of a gem reflects light differently, every perspective offers a distinct interpretation of situations, problems, and opportunities.

Enriching Creativity and Innovation

Homogeneity often leads to linear thinking. Diverse perspectives, with their multifaceted viewpoints, pave the way for innovative solutions. Different backgrounds bring varied problem-solving methodologies, creating a melting pot of ideas where creativity flourishes.

Comprehensive Problem Solving

A problem viewed from multiple angles is more likely to be understood in its entirety. Diverse perspectives ensure that every aspect of an issue is scrutinized, leading to well-rounded solutions. It's akin to gathering puzzle pieces from different sources to get a complete picture.

The Power of Empathy and Inclusion

Exposure to diverse perspectives nurtures empathy. When individuals are attuned to varied viewpoints, they become more understanding and less judgmental. This empathy not only fosters inclusivity within teams or communities but also helps in better serving a diverse clientele or population.

A Guard Against Myopia and Bias

Having a singular perspective can lead to myopia and inherent biases. A collection of diverse viewpoints acts as a check against these biases, ensuring that decisions are holistic and not skewed by singular experiences or beliefs.

Enhancing Decision-making Processes

Decision-making, especially in complex scenarios, benefits immensely from diverse insights. A range of perspectives ensures that decisions are robust, well-considered, and cater to a broad spectrum of needs and challenges.

Reflecting the Global Melting Pot

Today's world is a mosaic of cultures, experiences, and aspirations. For businesses, communities, or institutions to be truly global, it's imperative that they resonate with this diversity. Having varied perspectives ensures alignment with global sensibilities, making endeavors more universally relatable and effective.

Diverse Perspectives in Leadership

Leaders with diverse perspectives or those who value them are more adaptable and versatile. They can navigate challenges with a broadened worldview, ensuring that their leadership is effective across different cultural and social landscapes.

Economic Value and Market Expansion

For businesses, diverse perspectives can be a goldmine. They bring insights into different market segments, consumer behaviors, and uncharted territories, paving the way for expansion, increased relevance, and enhanced profitability.

Nurturing Continuous Learning and Growth

Exposure to varied perspectives is an education in itself. It breaks the shackles of routine thought processes, introduces new paradigms, and fosters a culture of continuous learning and personal growth.

Challenges in Harnessing Diverse Perspectives

While the value of diverse perspectives is undeniable, it's not without challenges. From potential misunderstandings, communication barriers, to resistance to change, diverse viewpoints can sometimes lead to friction. However, with conscious efforts, open dialogues, and a culture of respect, these challenges can be transformed into growth opportunities.

The Future Landscape:Increasing Interdependence of Diverse Perspectives

As the world becomes more interconnected, the interdependence on diverse perspectives will only amplify. Whether it's addressing global challenges, forging international collaborations, or creating products for a global audience, varied viewpoints will be at the heart of future successes.

In Conclusion

Diverse perspectives, in their richness, hold the key to a world of possibilities. They are not just valuable; they are essential. In their resonance lies the promise of a world that's more inclusive, innovative, empathetic, and holistic. By valuing and incorporating these myriad viewpoints, we pave the way for a future that's not just successful, but also harmonious and enlightened.

Chapter 3
Innovation & Creativity

Innovation and creativity serve as the lifeblood of progress, driving industries, businesses, and societies towards new horizons. By understanding their essence, dynamics, and interplay, we can harness their potential to craft groundbreaking solutions and envision futures previously unimagined.

The Distinction Between Innovation and Creativity

While they often walk hand-in-hand, creativity and innovation are not the same. Creativity is the act of conceiving new and original ideas, while innovation is the process of implementing these ideas into practical solutions. Think of creativity as the spark and innovation as the fire that results from fueling that spark.

The Wellspring of Creativity

Creativity thrives where minds are open, curious, and unafraid. It's nurtured by diverse experiences, continuous learning, and a willingness to challenge the status quo. From the depths of solitude to bustling collaborative spaces, creativity springs forth from various environments.

Innovation: The Structured Side of the Coin

Innovation takes the abstract and makes it tangible. It demands a structured approach: ideation, testing, modification, and implementation. Successful innovation isn't just about novel ideas; it's about ensuring they're viable, scalable, and address real-world challenges.

The Synergy of Collaboration in Boosting Creativity

The blending of different perspectives often results in an explosion of creative ideas. Environments where collaboration is celebrated become hotbeds for creative thinking. Through the exchange of ideas and brainstorming, teams can discover new pathways and solutions.

Cultivating a Culture of Innovation

An innovative culture is more than just a buzzword. It requires fostering an environment where risks are tolerated, failures are seen as learning opportunities, and out-of-the-box thinking is encouraged. From top-tier management to entry-level positions, everyone must be aligned with this culture.

The Role of Limitations in Sparking Creativity

Contrary to popular belief, limitations often act as catalysts for creativity. When resources are scarce or challenges appear insurmountable, it forces individuals and teams to think differently, to approach problems with a fresh mindset, and to find unconventional solutions.

Digital Age: Amplifying the Potential for Innovation

The digital revolution has exponentially magnified the arena for innovation. With tools like AI, big data analytics, and cloud computing, there's an array of possibilities for crafting innovative solutions. Moreover, the digital era has democratized innovation, giving voices and platforms to those previously unheard.

Learning from Creative and Innovative Failures

Not every creative idea will result in successful innovation. Some will falter at the ideation stage, others during implementation. However, these failures, when analyzed, offer invaluable insights. They teach resilience, adaptability, and the art of pivoting.

Future Trajectories: Where are Creativity and Innovation Heading?

As the world grapples with unprecedented challenges, from climate change to evolving societal dynamics, the demand for creativity and innovation has never been more acute. The future will witness a surge in interdisciplinary collaborations, where varied skill sets converge to design holistic solutions.

The Ethical Dimensions of Innovation

Innovation, especially when fueled by technological advancements, can sometimes outpace ethical considerations. It's imperative to introspect: Just because we can innovate, should we? Balancing innovation with ethical considerations ensures sustainable and responsible progress.

Nurturing Personal Creativity and Driving Self-Innovation

While organizational creativity and innovation are often discussed, personal creativity and self-innovation are equally crucial. Cultivating habits like continuous learning, mindfulness, exposure to diverse experiences, and reflection can significantly boost one's creative and innovative capacities.

Real-world Case Studies: From Ideation to Implementation

Analyzing real-world instances of successful (and unsuccessful) creativity and innovation offers practical insights. Whether it's Apple's tryst with user-centric design or Blockbuster's inability to innovate in the face of digital streaming, these case studies provide rich learning opportunities.

In Conclusion

Creativity and innovation, in their dance, hold the promise of a brighter, more advanced, and more empathetic world. By understanding their nuances and fostering environments where they can thrive, individuals, organizations, and societies can propel themselves into realms of progress previously deemed unreachable. The journey from the spark of a creative idea to the roaring flame of successful innovation is intricate, challenging, but above all, incredibly rewarding.

Pioneering the Future

In a world marked by rapid technological advances, shifting societal norms, and pressing environmental challenges, there is a pressing need for pioneers. These are individuals and collectives willing to take risks, challenge the status quo, and chart the course for a brighter future. Pioneering is more than just innovating; it's about envisioning a new world and being instrumental in its creation.

The Essence of Pioneering

At its core, pioneering is about venturing into uncharted territories. Historically, pioneers were explorers who discovered new lands, but in today's context, it signifies those who break boundaries in thought, technology, or societal norms to usher in a new era.

The Evolutionary Imperative of Pioneering

As species evolve, they adapt to ever-changing environments. In the human realm, pioneering is an evolutionary imperative, ensuring that we not only adapt but thrive amidst change. From harnessing fire to the digital revolution, pioneers have consistently driven human progress.

The Psyche of a Pioneer

What makes someone a pioneer? It's a blend of innate curiosity, indomitable will, and the courage to face the unknown. A pioneer sees challenges as opportunities and is often willing to take paths less traveled, driven by conviction and a vision.

Pioneering and Technological Revolutions

Every technological leap, from the printing press to the internet, owes its success to pioneers. These are people who visualized a different world, where new tools redefine human capabilities and societal structures. In today's context, pioneers in AI, quantum computing, and biotechnology are crafting futures we can scarcely imagine.

Societal and Cultural Frontiers

Pioneering isn't limited to technology. There are pioneers in art, culture, and social thought, challenging stereotypes, breaking barriers, and redefining what's possible. Be it the suffragettes of the early 20th century or the champions of LGBTQ+ rights in recent decades, these pioneers reshape societal landscapes.

The Environmental Vanguard

As the Earth grapples with climate change and ecological imbalance, pioneers in sustainability are crucial. They envision a world where humans live in harmony with nature. Through innovative solutions like renewable energy, sustainable agriculture, and conservation efforts, these pioneers are scripting a greener, more sustainable future.

The Challenges Pioneers Face

Pioneering is not without its trials. Pioneers often face resistance from the status quo, skepticism, and sometimes outright hostility. Their ideas, being ahead of their time, may be ridiculed or dismissed. Yet, it's their resilience and belief in their vision that propels them forward.

The Interplay of Tradition and Pioneering

While pioneering is about breaking boundaries, it's also about understanding and respecting traditions. Often, the most impactful pioneers are those who weave the wisdom of the past into their vision for the future, ensuring continuity even in the face of radical change.

Pioneering in Leadership: Steering Ships into the Unknown

Great leaders are often pioneers, navigating their teams, organizations, or even nations through uncharted waters. Their leadership style is marked by adaptability, vision, and the ability to inspire trust even when the destination is uncertain.

The Ethics of Pioneering

With the power to reshape worlds, pioneering also carries ethical responsibilities. How do pioneers ensure that their innovations and ideas benefit humanity at large and not just a select few? The balance between progress and ethical considerations is a tightrope that every pioneer must walk.

Nurturing the Next Generation of Pioneers

What does it take to nurture future pioneers? A blend of education, exposure to diverse thoughts, encouragement to challenge established norms, and most importantly, cultivating the belief that change is not only possible but imperative.

The Legacy of Pioneers: Beyond Their Time

Pioneers, through their thoughts, innovations, and actions, leave a lasting legacy. They might be ahead of their time, but their contributions resonate through ages, influencing generations and shaping the course of history.

In Conclusion

Pioneering the future is a lofty and daunting task. It demands courage, vision, resilience, and a profound sense of responsibility. As we stand on the cusp of numerous changes, from technological revolutions to societal shifts, the role of pioneers becomes ever more crucial. They hold the torch, illuminating the path for the rest of humanity, ensuring that as we step into the unknown, we do so with hope, purpose, and the promise of a better tomorrow.

Inspirational Quotes on Innovation

Innovation is the driving force behind progress, pushing boundaries and inspiring change in every aspect of human life. Quotes encapsulate the essence of innovation, providing bite-sized wisdom that can be referred to for motivation and direction. In this exploration, we'll delve into several inspirational quotes on innovation, dissecting their meanings and relevance for various contexts.

"Innovation distinguishes between a leader and a follower."

- *Steve Jobs*

Explanation

Jobs believed that the ability to innovate separated those who merely followed trends from those who set them. Leaders, in his eyes, are visionaries who aren't afraid to challenge the status quo and introduce novel ideas. This quote serves as a call to action for aspiring leaders, urging them to embrace innovation as a cornerstone of effective leadership.

"There's a way to do it better—find it."

- *Thomas Edison*

Explanation

Edison, with his vast array of inventions, was a testament to the belief that there's always room for improvement. His quote resonates with innovators by reminding them that complacency is innovation's adversary. No matter how effective a solution might seem, there's likely a more efficient or innovative approach waiting to be discovered.

"You can't solve a problem on the same level that it was created. You have to rise above it to the next level."

- *Albert Einstein*

Explanation

Einstein emphasizes the need for a fresh perspective when addressing challenges. True innovation often requires stepping out of the familiar, reframing the problem, and exploring it from new angles. This approach often yields groundbreaking solutions that would otherwise remain undiscovered.

"The only way to discover the limits of the possible is to go beyond them into the impossible."

- *Arthur C. Clarke*

Explanation

Clarke, a science fiction writer, believed in pushing boundaries. His quote encourages risk-taking and exploration, suggesting that true innovation arises when one dares to venture into uncharted territories, even if they seem improbable.

"Innovation is seeing what everybody has seen and thinking what nobody has thought."

- *Dr. Albert Szent-Györgyi*

Explanation

Innovation isn't necessarily about inventing something entirely new. Instead, it's about perceiving existing scenarios or tools in a unique way. This quote is a testament to the power of perspective, urging individuals to view the familiar with fresh eyes.

"Innovation is the calling card of the future."

- Anna Eshoo

Explanation: Eshoo's words highlight the significance of innovation in shaping the future. As societies and technologies evolve, those who innovate are the ones who define the trajectory of progress. In essence, today's innovators are architects of tomorrow's world.

"Minds are like parachutes - they only function when open."

- Thomas Dewar

Explanation

Dewar uses a witty analogy to underline the importance of an open mind. For innovation to occur, one must be receptive to new ideas, unburdened by biases or preconceived notions. A closed mind, like a shut parachute, is of little use and can even be detrimental.

"The value of an idea lies in the using of it."

- Thomas Edison

Explanation

Ideas in isolation hold limited value. Edison's quote emphasizes the translation of ideas into actionable solutions or products. It's a reminder that innovation isn't just about creativity; it's equally about execution.

"If you always do what you always did, you will always get what you always got."

- Albert Einstein

Explanation

Einstein's words are a warning against the pitfalls of stagnation. Routine and repetitiveness can hinder progress. To achieve different outcomes and foster innovation, one must be willing to change tactics, strategies, or viewpoints.

"Innovation is about turning ideas into real things."

- Tom Kelly

Explanation

Kelly's quote reiterates that innovation is a tangible process. It's not just about brainstorming or ideation; it's about realizing those concepts in the real world. Innovators bridge the gap between the abstract and the concrete.

In Conclusion

Innovation is an intricate dance of creativity, risk-taking, execution, and vision. These quotes, each profound in its own right, provide a roadmap for aspiring innovators, offering insights and encouragement. They remind us that innovation is often a challenging journey, fraught with failures and uncertainties, but the rewards, both personal and societal, are immense. In the ever-evolving tapestry of human history, innovation serves as the thread pushing us towards brighter horizons, and these pearls of wisdom light the way.

Encouraging Creativity in the Workplace

In today's competitive business environment, companies are constantly searching for a unique edge to stand out and sustain growth. One such avenue that can significantly drive success is fostering a culture of creativity. But why is creativity important, and how can businesses practically encourage and harness it in the workplace? Let's explore.

Understanding Creativity

At its essence, creativity is about viewing the world differently, finding new solutions to problems, and generating novel ideas. Contrary to common belief, it's not limited to the arts but spans every aspect of business, from product development and marketing to strategy and human resources.

The Importance of Creativity in Business

Problem-Solving

Unique problems require unique solutions. Creative thinking enables teams to approach challenges from various angles, leading to more comprehensive and innovative solutions.

Competitive Advantage

Companies that consistently innovate set themselves apart in the market. Think Apple's user-friendly designs or Tesla's approach to electric vehicles.

Adaptability

In an ever-changing business environment, a creative workforce can pivot more easily, adapting products, services, or strategies in response to unforeseen challenges.

Creating a Conducive Environment

Physical Space

An open, vibrant, and flexible workspace can stimulate the mind. Google's offices, with their breakout spaces, relaxation pods, and themed rooms, are designed to spark creativity.

Diverse Teams

Diversity isn't just about ticking boxes. Diverse teams bring a range of perspectives, experiences, and ideas, leading to richer brainstorming sessions and more innovative solutions.

Training and Workshops

Regular workshops emphasizing creative thinking can equip employees with tools to think outside the box. This includes training in areas like design thinking or lateral thinking.

Leadership's Role

Lead by Example

Leaders should exemplify creative thinking. This might mean presenting novel solutions, encouraging diverse opinions, or simply showing a willingness to take calculated risks.

Open Communication Channels

Hierarchical systems can stifle creativity. Leaders should cultivate an open-door policy, encouraging employees at all levels to share their ideas.

Reward Innovation

Recognizing and rewarding innovative ideas reinforces their importance. This could be through bonuses, public acknowledgment, or even giving teams the resources to turn their creative concepts into reality.

Overcoming Barriers to Creativity

Fear of Failure

The fear of making mistakes can be crippling. Companies should foster a culture where failure is seen as a stepping stone to success, a necessary part of the innovation process.

Time Constraints

While it's crucial to meet deadlines, employees should also have the liberty to take a step back, reflect, and let their creative juices flow without constantly watching the clock.

Lack of Resources

Not every creative idea requires a huge budget. Sometimes, constraints can even spur creativity. However, ensuring teams have the tools and resources they need is pivotal.

Tools and Techniques

Brainstorming Sessions

Regular sessions where team members can throw around ideas without judgment can lead to unexpected and innovative solutions.

Mind Mapping

This visual tool can help teams organize thoughts, see connections, and expand on ideas, fostering creativity in project planning or problem-solving.

Feedback Loops

Constant feedback, both positive and constructive, can refine ideas and encourage their evolution.

The Link Between Well-being and Creativity

Employee well-being directly impacts creativity. A stressed or overworked individual is less likely to think creatively. Companies can:

Promote Work-Life Balance

Ensure employees aren't overburdened, and they have adequate time to recharge.

Mental Health Initiatives

Programs focusing on mental health can keep employees in a positive frame of mind, conducive to creativity.

Encourage Vacations and Breaks

Time away from the daily grind can offer fresh perspectives and rejuvenate the mind.

Continuous Evolution

Feedback and Review

Implement regular feedback mechanisms to understand what's working and what isn't in your quest to foster creativity.

Stay Updated

The world of business is dynamic. Regular training sessions and workshops can keep the workforce updated, equipped with the latest tools and techniques to fuel their creative minds.

In Conclusion

Creativity is not just a buzzword; it's a tangible asset that can propel businesses forward. By fostering a culture of creativity, companies don't merely survive; they thrive, innovate, and lead. Encouraging creativity in the workplace requires a concerted effort, from leadership's commitment to creating a conducive environment and equipping teams with the right tools. The payoff, however, in terms of groundbreaking solutions, a motivated workforce, and a distinct market position, makes it an investment worth making.

Chapter 4
Decision Making & Strategy

Decision-making is the beating heart of any organization. It steers the ship, determining direction, strategy, and ultimate success or failure. As the business landscape evolves, so too must our approaches to making decisions and crafting strategy. This chapter delves into the intricacies of decision-making and strategy, offering insights into best practices, common pitfalls, and the modern tools and frameworks that guide today's most successful enterprises.

The Essence of Decision Making

Decision-making is more than just choosing between options. It's a systematic process of defining problems, evaluating alternatives, and selecting the best course of action. In a business context, decisions range from day-to-day operational choices to strategic determinations that define the organization's future.

Strategic Decision Making

Strategic decisions lay the groundwork for a company's long-term direction and vision. They require a deep understanding of the business, its environment, and its potential trajectory. These decisions often involve a higher level of uncertainty and risk but carry the potential for significant rewards.

Frameworks for Decision Making

SWOT Analysis

A simple yet effective tool, SWOT Analysis examines a company's Strengths, Weaknesses, Opportunities, and Threats. It's instrumental in aligning organizational strengths with opportunities while mitigating weaknesses and threats.

PESTEL Analysis

This tool evaluates external factors (Political, Economic, Social, Technological, Environmental, and Legal) that might affect an organization, assisting in proactive strategy development.

The Decision Matrix

A quantitative method to rank and evaluate options based on specific criteria, providing a structured approach to making complex decisions.

Strategy Formulation: Crafting a Vision

Strategies are the broad plans organizations employ to achieve their objectives. Effective strategies are:

Aligned with Vision and Mission

The company's overarching goals should guide strategy.

Adaptable

Given the dynamic business environment, strategies should be flexible enough to adapt to unforeseen changes.

Inclusive

Input from various stakeholders, including employees, shareholders, and even customers, can enrich strategy formulation.

Balancing Data with Intuition

While data-driven decision-making is all the rage, there's something to be said for intuition, especially when navigating uncharted waters. The most effective leaders often strike a balance:

Data Analysis

Utilizing metrics, analytics, and research to inform decisions.

Gut Feeling

Sometimes, past experiences, industry insights, and an inherent sense of direction guide decisions where data might be lacking.

Avoiding Common Decision-making Pitfalls

Analysis Paralysis

Overanalyzing can lead to decision-making delays. It's essential to strike a balance between thorough analysis and timely action.

Confirmation Bias

Leaders must avoid the trap of only seeking out information that confirms their preconceived notions.

Groupthink

Encouraging diverse opinions and challenging the status quo can prevent the perils of groupthink.

The Role of Feedback

Feedback loops, both internal (from teams) and external (from customers or clients), are vital. They provide:

Validation

Feedback can confirm if a decision or strategy is effective.

Course Correction

Early feedback can highlight potential issues, allowing for quick pivots.

The Future of Decision Making and Strategy

AI and Machine Learning

Advanced algorithms can process vast amounts of data at unprecedented speeds, offering insights and predictive models that can significantly inform decisions.

Crowdsourcing

Tapping into the collective intelligence of a broad audience, be it employees, customers, or the general public, can bring fresh perspectives and innovative solutions.

Evaluating Decisions

Post-decision evaluations are as crucial as the decision-making process itself. They involve:

Performance Metrics

Tracking the outcomes against predefined benchmarks.

Stakeholder Feedback

Understanding the impacts of decisions on various stakeholders.

Reflection and Learning

Analyzing what went right, what went wrong, and how to improve in the future.

In Conclusion

Decision-making and strategy formulation, while challenging, are what differentiate successful organizations from their peers. They require a harmonious blend of analytical rigor, intuition, foresight, and adaptability. In a world marked by rapid changes and increasing complexities, leaders equipped with the right tools, frameworks, and mindsets will steer their organizations towards sustained success and growth.

Navigating Business Choices

Every business, irrespective of its size or industry, faces a multitude of choices daily. These decisions can range from trivial to transformative, with some potentially altering the very trajectory of the company. This chapter aims to shine a light on the process, complexities, and best practices associated with navigating business choices.

The Multifaceted Nature of Business Choices

Every choice made within a business context is shaped by a myriad of factors:

Stakeholder Interests

Decisions often have to balance the varied interests of shareholders, employees, customers, and society at large.

Economic Conditions

The broader economic climate, from interest rates to global market trends, can heavily influence business choices.

Company Culture and Values

The internal ethos of a company often acts as a guiding principle for decisions.

The Spectrum of Business Choices

Business choices span a wide spectrum:

Operational Choices

Day-to-day decisions related to the functioning of the business. Examples include inventory management or shift scheduling.

Strategic Choices

Long-term decisions that define the direction and vision of the company, such as mergers, acquisitions, or entry into new markets.

Ethical Choices

Decisions centered around moral considerations, like sustainable sourcing or fair labor practices.

Structured Decision-making Processes

Given the complexity and stakes involved, businesses cannot afford to approach choices haphazardly. A structured process often involves:

Problem Definition

Clearly identifying and articulating the issue at hand.

Information Gathering

Collecting relevant data and insights to inform the decision.

Evaluation

Weighing various options based on their merits and potential impacts.

Implementation

Enacting the chosen decision.

Review

Assessing the outcomes and refining the approach if necessary.

Tools to Aid Decision Making

In a world awash with data, various tools and frameworks assist in making informed choices

Cost-Benefit Analysis

Assessing the potential benefits of a decision against its associated costs.

Decision Trees

A visual representation of possible outcomes, pathways, and choices.

Scenario Planning

Forecasting different potential futures to understand the implications of choices in various contexts.

Emotional Intelligence and Decision Making

While data and logical frameworks are invaluable, the importance of emotional intelligence (EQ) in decision-making can't be understated

Empathy

Understanding and considering the emotional and human impact of decisions.

Self-Awareness

Recognizing one's biases and emotions that might cloud judgment.

Relationship Management

Ensuring decisions foster positive relations with stakeholders.

The Paradox of Choice

In some instances, having too many options can be paralyzing, leading to decision fatigue and potential inaction:

Overcome Overanalysis

While thorough analysis is crucial, it's equally vital to recognize when it's time to decide.

Simplify Choices

Where possible, streamline options to make the decision-making process more manageable.

Navigating Ethical Choices

Businesses today are under the spotlight more than ever, with stakeholders demanding ethical and responsible behavior:

Stakeholder Engagement

Regular dialogues with stakeholders can offer insights into their values and concerns.

Ethical Frameworks

Adopting established ethical frameworks can guide businesses during moral dilemmas.

Transparency

Openly communicating the rationale behind decisions, especially contentious ones, can foster trust and understanding.

Learning from Mistakes

No decision-making process is foolproof. Mistakes are inevitable, but they offer invaluable learning opportunities:

Feedback Loops

Establishing mechanisms to gather feedback on decisions can highlight areas of improvement.

Cultivating a Growth Mindset

Viewing errors as growth opportunities, rather than failures, can foster a culture of continuous improvement.

The Future of Business Decision Making

As businesses evolve, so too will the nature and complexity of the choices they face

Artificial Intelligence

AI offers the potential to analyze vast datasets, offering insights and recommendations at unprecedented speeds.

Collaborative Decision Making

As businesses become more interconnected and global, decisions will increasingly involve collaborations between various entities.

In Conclusion

Navigating business choices is a complex dance, balancing logic with emotion, immediate needs with long-term vision, and individual interests with collective goals. As the business landscape continues to evolve, companies that approach decisions with a blend of data-driven insights, emotional intelligence, and ethical considerations will be best poised to thrive and make a positive impact.

Strategic Quotes for Success

Quotes have always served as encapsulations of wisdom, motivation, and insights across various domains. When it comes to business, they can guide leaders, inspire teams, and help shape organizational direction. This chapter aims to explore the power and influence of strategic quotes, dissecting their profound implications for driving success in business.

The Importance of Quotes in Business Strategy

Strategic quotes are more than mere words. They represent:

Timeless Wisdom

These nuggets of knowledge often stem from tried and tested experiences.

A Source of Motivation

A well-placed quote can inspire teams, especially during challenging times.

Guiding Principles

They can act as compasses, keeping businesses aligned with their vision.

Leadership and Vision

"Management is doing things right; leadership is doing the right things."

- Peter F. Drucker

This quote underscores the distinction between mere management and true leadership. While management emphasizes efficiency and processes, leadership delves deeper into guiding an organization with purpose and vision.

Embracing Change and Innovation

"The only thing that is constant is change."

- Heraclitus

In a rapidly evolving business landscape, this ancient quote remains eerily relevant. Companies that remain static risk obsolescence. Embracing change, while challenging, is fundamental to continuous growth and innovation.

Perseverance and Resilience

"Success is not final, failure is not fatal: It is the courage to continue that counts."

- Winston Churchill

Churchill's words serve as a poignant reminder that success and failure are but transient states in the business world. What truly distinguishes enduring companies is their resilience and tenacity.

Integrity and Ethics

"The supreme quality for leadership is unquestionably integrity. Without it, no real success is possible."

- Dwight D. Eisenhower

Eisenhower highlights the pivotal role of integrity in leadership. As businesses face increasing scrutiny from stakeholders, ethical considerations are paramount to long-term success and reputation.

Teamwork and Collaboration

"Alone we can do so little; together we can do so much."

- Helen Keller

Keller's words echo the significance of collaboration. In a business context, silos can be detrimental. Companies that foster a culture of teamwork often unlock innovative solutions and attain greater accomplishments.

Continuous Learning

"The capacity to learn is a gift; the ability to learn is a skill; the willingness to learn is a choice."

- Brian Herbert

In an age of information, continuous learning sets apart forward-thinking businesses. This quote emphasizes that while everyone has the potential to learn, it's the proactive choice to do so that distinguishes the truly successful.

Decisiveness and Action

"In any moment of decision, the best thing you can do is the right thing, the next best thing is the wrong thing, and the worst thing you can do is nothing."

- Theodore Roosevelt

Roosevelt's insight highlights the importance of action over inaction. Even missteps, when approached correctly, can be turned into learning opportunities.

Value Creation

"Price is what you pay. Value is what you get."

- Warren Buffett

Buffett, one of the most successful investors, underscores the distinction between cost and value. In business, the focus should always be on delivering unparalleled value to stakeholders.

Adapting to the Marketplace

"Business has only two functions – marketing and innovation."

- Milan Kundera

Kundera aptly summarizes the core functions of any business. To thrive, companies must innovate and effectively communicate their value propositions to the marketplace.

Reflection on Past Wisdom for Future Success

Strategic quotes often encapsulate age-old wisdom that remains relevant across generations. By reflecting on these insights, businesses can:

Avoid Past Mistakes

Historical wisdom provides cautionary tales, allowing modern businesses to sidestep previous pitfalls.

Reinforce Core Values

Amidst rapid changes, timeless quotes act as anchors, reminding businesses of their core principles and values.

Incorporating Quotes in Business Strategy

Training and Workshops

Use quotes to underscore key points during corporate training.

Company Literature

Imbue company reports, presentations, and marketing materials with relevant quotes for emphasis.

Team Meetings

Start or end meetings with a quote to set the tone or provide closure.

In Conclusion

Strategic quotes, with their condensed wisdom, provide businesses with insights, motivation, and guidance. They remind us of time-tested principles, encourage reflection, and inspire action. As businesses navigate the complexities of the modern world, these quotes serve as beacons, illuminating the path to success.

The Role of Intuition in Business

Intuition, often dubbed as the "gut feeling," has long been a topic of interest and discussion in the realm of business. While some consider intuition to be an unreliable and unscientific approach, others view it as an invaluable tool that complements analytical thinking. This chapter aims to delve into the role of intuition in business, exploring its merits, pitfalls, and optimal application.

Understanding Intuition

Intuition can be described as an instinctive, immediate understanding or knowing without the conscious use of reasoning. It's the visceral response or "hunch" that doesn't always come with logical backing but feels compelling nonetheless.

Origins

Rooted in our evolutionary history, intuition is believed to have served our ancestors in making quick decisions in life-threatening situations.

Subconscious Processing

While intuition feels instantaneous, it often results from rapid subconscious processing based on past experiences and learned patterns.

Intuition vs. Analytical Thinking

Speed

Intuition provides quick, almost instantaneous answers, while analytical thinking is a slower, step-by-step process.

Basis

Intuitive decisions are based on feelings and past experiences, while analytical decisions are based on logical reasoning and evidence.

Reliability

Analytical thinking is often considered more reliable as it can be verified with data, whereas intuition is more subjective.

The Merits of Intuition in Business

Quick Decision-making

In situations that require swift action, intuition can guide leaders to make prompt decisions without paralysis by analysis.

Reading People

Human interactions, like negotiations or hiring decisions, often benefit from intuitive readings of individuals' intentions and character.

Navigating Uncertainty

In uncharted territories where data may be lacking, intuition can act as a guiding light.

The Pitfalls of Relying Solely on Intuition

Bias and Misjudgment

Intuition can be tainted by personal biases, leading to flawed decisions.

Lack of Reproducibility

Decisions based purely on intuition can be hard to justify or reproduce, making them less transparent to stakeholders.

Potential for Overconfidence

A history of successful intuitive decisions can make leaders overconfident, sidelining analytical assessment.

Balancing Intuition with Analysis

For optimal decision-making, businesses should strive to strike a balance:

Gather Data

Always start with gathering relevant data and performing an analytical assessment.

Check with Your Gut

After a logical assessment, consult your intuitive feelings about the situation.

Iterative Feedback

Use the outcomes of decisions to refine both intuitive and analytical skills.

Cultivating Intuition in Business

Experience

The richness of intuition often correlates with the breadth and depth of experiences. Exposure to diverse business scenarios can sharpen intuitive faculties.

Reflection

Regularly reflecting on past decisions, both intuitive and analytical, can hone decision-making skills.

Mindfulness Practices

Techniques like meditation can heighten self-awareness and enhance intuitive capabilities.

Intuition in Innovation

Innovators like Steve Jobs swore by intuition. In realms like product design or branding, intuitive insights can capture the unspoken needs and desires of the market.

Going Beyond Data

While market research provides a baseline, true innovation often requires looking beyond numbers to intuitively grasp consumer desires.

Risks and Rewards

Intuitive decisions in innovation come with their fair share of risks but can yield groundbreaking rewards.

Real-world Examples of Intuition in Business

Oprah Winfrey

Her intuitive understanding of human emotions and stories turned her show into a cultural phenomenon.

George Soros

The financial magnate often spoke of using his "gut feelings" alongside analytical methods in investment decisions.

The Future of Intuition in an Age of Data

With the rise of Big Data and AI, there's a valid concern: Will intuition become obsolete?

Data Overload

Paradoxically, the sheer volume of data today can make analytical decisions more challenging, accentuating the need for intuitive clarity.

The Human Touch

While machines excel in analysis, the intuitive understanding of human emotions, desires, and motivations remains a uniquely human domain.

In Conclusion

Intuition, while intangible and often elusive, holds a distinctive place in the business realm. It complements analytical thinking, enabling leaders to navigate complex terrains, understand people deeply, and innovate beyond the obvious. As the business landscape evolves, fostering a harmonious blend of intuition and analysis will be pivotal for enduring success.

Chapter 5
Ethics & Integrity

In the corporate world, where the bottom line often takes precedence, the significance of ethics and integrity cannot be overstated. These two principles lay the foundation for sustainable business practices, foster trust with stakeholders, and create a legacy that transcends profit margins. This chapter delves deep into the roles of ethics and integrity in business, elucidating their importance, implications, and methods of incorporation.

Defining Ethics and Integrity

Ethics

Refers to the moral principles that guide the decisions and actions of an individual or group. It's about distinguishing between right and wrong based on societal and personal values.

Integrity

Is about consistency in actions, values, methods, and principles. It signifies honesty and truthfulness in all business dealings.

The Significance of Ethics and Integrity in Business

Trust Building

Ethical businesses cultivate trust among their stakeholders – customers, employees, and investors.

Reputation Management

Companies known for their integrity are more resilient against scandals and negative publicity.

Long-term Success

While unethical practices might offer short-term gains, only businesses grounded in ethics and integrity achieve lasting success.

Ethics, Integrity, and the Bottom Line

Sustainable Profitability

Ethical companies often enjoy customer loyalty, which translates to sustained profitability.

Avoiding Litigation

Adherence to ethical standards can prevent costly lawsuits and regulatory fines.

Employee Satisfaction

A company that values ethics and integrity attracts and retains top talent, leading to increased productivity.

The Global Implications of Business Ethics

Fair Trade

Ethical businesses ensure that they source products under fair conditions, promoting better living standards for suppliers.

Environmental Responsibility

Ethical decision-making includes considering the environmental impact, leading to sustainable business practices.

Cross-cultural Respect

As businesses go global, respecting and understanding diverse cultures becomes paramount.

The Challenges of Maintaining Integrity

Short-term Pressures

The pressure to meet quarterly targets can sometimes push businesses to compromise on their ethical standards.

Competitive Markets

In fiercely competitive markets, the temptation to cut corners can challenge a company's integrity.

Cultural Differences

Navigating business ethics in a global context can be challenging due to differing cultural perceptions of right and wrong.

Incorporating Ethics and Integrity into Company Culture

Leadership By Example

Senior leadership should embody the company's ethical principles in their actions.

Clear Codes of Conduct

Clearly defined ethical guidelines help employees understand and adhere to the company's values.

Regular Training

Periodic workshops can keep the importance of ethics and integrity fresh in employees' minds.

Whistleblowing and Ethical Vigilance

Encouraging Reporting

Employees should feel safe reporting unethical behaviors without fear of retaliation.

Third-party Oversight

External audits and oversight can help maintain a company's ethical standards.

Real-world Cases of Ethical Dilemmas

Enron Scandal

A case that underscores the catastrophic consequences of forsaking ethics for short-term gains.

Volkswagen Emissions Scandal

Demonstrates the long-term reputational and financial costs of unethical corporate decisions.

The Ethical Consumer and the Role of Integrity in Branding

Consumer Awareness

Today's consumers are more informed and value brands that prioritize ethical business practices.

Transparency

Brands that are transparent about their processes and values tend to garner more trust.

Authenticity

Consumers can differentiate between genuine brand values and mere marketing tactics. Authenticity, rooted in real ethical practices, is key.

The Future of Ethics and Integrity in Business

Technological Considerations

As AI and data analytics play larger roles in businesses, new ethical considerations emerge.

Increased Accountability

With the rise of social media, businesses are more accountable to the public than ever before.

Stakeholder Expectations

Modern stakeholders, including investors, expect businesses to prioritize ethics alongside profitability.

In Conclusion

Ethics and integrity are more than just buzzwords or checkboxes in an annual report. They are foundational pillars upon which successful, sustainable, and respected businesses are built. In a rapidly evolving global economy, these values not only protect companies from potential pitfalls but also position them as leaders and pioneers. Companies that prioritize ethics and integrity pave the way for a brighter, more responsible business future.

The Backbone of Trust

Trust is not just an abstract ideal or a simple word thrown around in conversations. In both personal relationships and business dealings, trust is the bedrock upon which all lasting interactions are built. When dissected, trust reveals itself as a complex tapestry of shared experiences, upheld promises, and consistent behavior. This chapter delves deep into the concept of trust, revealing why it's vital, how it's cultivated, and its lasting impacts.

Defining Trust

Trust as a Belief

At its core, trust is a firm belief in the reliability, truth, ability, or strength of someone or something.

The Dimensions of Trust

Trust isn't one-dimensional. It encompasses predictability, dependability, and faith, each playing a unique role.

The Psychological Foundations of Trust

Safety and Security: Humans are wired to seek out safety. Trust indicates a belief in a predictable outcome, providing emotional security.

Past as a Predictor

Past interactions and experiences greatly influence the propensity to trust. Positive past interactions often lead to a higher likelihood of trust in the future.

Trust in Personal Relationships

The Building Blocks

Small acts, consistent behavior, and open communication lay the groundwork for trust in interpersonal relationships.

Repairing Broken Trust

Trust, once broken, is challenging to restore. It demands acknowledgment of mistakes, genuine remorse, and consistent efforts to rebuild.

The Pivotal Role of Trust in Business

Employee Trust

Employees who trust their employers are more motivated, loyal, and productive.

Consumer Trust

Brands that earn the trust of their consumers enjoy higher loyalty, better word of mouth, and increased sales.

B2B Trust

In business-to-business dealings, trust ensures smoother collaborations, longer contracts, and mutual growth.

Trust as a Tangible Asset

Monetary Value of Trust

Brands that are trusted often have a higher market value and can command premium prices.

Trust Deficit: A lack of trust can lead to decreased sales, higher operational costs due to oversight mechanisms, and decreased brand value.

Cultivating Trust in Business

Transparency: Being open about processes, especially in times of crises, helps build trust.

Consistency

Delivering consistently on promises and maintaining product or service quality is key.

Open Feedback Channels

Allowing and addressing feedback indicates that a business values its customers and is willing to improve.

Trust in the Digital Age

Online Reviews and Trust

In today's digital world, online reviews play a significant role in building or breaking trust.

Data Privacy and Trust

Companies that protect user data and are transparent about its usage earn users' trust.

Social Media's Double-Edged Sword

While social media can amplify trust through positive testimonials, it can also rapidly disseminate instances of broken trust.

The Global Implications of Trust

Cross-cultural Trust-building

As businesses go global, understanding cultural nuances becomes essential in building trust.

Trust in Global Politics

Trust between nations can lead to peaceful relations, trade agreements, and collaborative innovations.

The Fragility and Resilience of Trust

The Domino Effect

One instance of breached trust can have cascading effects, affecting various facets of a relationship or business.

Restoring Trust

While rebuilding trust is challenging, it's not impossible. It requires time, genuine efforts, and often third-party interventions or guarantees.

Trust as a Continuous Journey

Evolving Dynamics

As situations change, the dynamics of trust also evolve. Continual efforts are required to maintain and grow trust.

The Iterative Process

Trust-building is an iterative process, demanding regular reflection, learning, and adaptation.

In Conclusion

Trust, often seen as intangible, is the very backbone of all sustainable interactions. Whether it's the trust a consumer places in their favorite brand or the trust between nations that paves the way for global collaborations, its importance cannot be overstated. In an era defined by rapid information exchange and digital interactions, trust remains the silent force driving loyalty, respect, and mutual growth. Investing in trust is not just a moral imperative but also a strategic one, promising long-term returns in harmony, collaboration, and prosperity.

Timeless Quotes on Integrity

Integrity, as a value, has been cherished and venerated across cultures, ages, and societies. Its importance transcends fleeting trends, underlining the timeless nature of upstanding character. Quotes, those succinct and powerful expressions of human thought, have often captured the essence of integrity in ways that volumes of books might sometimes fail to. This chapter delves deep into some timeless quotes on integrity, offering reflections on their profound meanings and applications.

Introduction to Integrity Through Quotes

Integrity is doing the right thing, even when no one is watching."

- C.S. Lewis

Reflection

This quote encapsulates the heart of integrity. It's not about public recognition but an innate moral compass that guides one's actions irrespective of external observation.

The Inherent Value of Integrity

"Our character is what we do when we think no one is looking."

- H. Jackson Brown Jr.

Reflection

Actions performed outside the spotlight, in anonymity, truly define our character. Integrity is about consistent ethics, not just those displayed publicly.

The Timelessness of Integrity

"Real integrity is doing the right thing, knowing that nobody's going to know whether you did it or not."

- Oprah Winfrey

Reflection

Winfrey emphasizes that genuine integrity is internal, an unwavering principle that doesn't change with time or audience.

Integrity as an Inner Compass

"Integrity is the essence of everything successful."

- R. Buckminster Fuller

Reflection

Fuller suggests that success devoid of integrity is fleeting. True success, enduring and meaningful, is deeply rooted in integrity.

The Immensity of Small Acts

"It is true that integrity alone won't make you a leader, but without integrity, you will never be one."

- Zig Ziglar

Reflection

While leadership requires multiple attributes, integrity is foundational. A leader without integrity lacks the moral authority to lead.

Integrity and Self-respect

"Self-respect is the cornerstone of all virtue."

- John Herschel

Reflection

Without self-respect, virtues like integrity are difficult to uphold. It's the self-respect that fuels one to act with integrity even in trying times.

The Costs and Rewards of Integrity

"There is no pillow so soft as a clear conscience."

- French Proverb

Reflection

This proverb highlights that the peace derived from a life of integrity is unparalleled. The comfort of knowing one acted rightly is a reward in itself.

Integrity as a Lifelong Commitment

"Character is much easier kept than recovered."

- Thomas Paine

Reflection

Once compromised, integrity is challenging to rebuild. It's a lifelong commitment and should be guarded zealously.

The Tangibility of Integrity

"Integrity is not something you show others. It is how you behave behind their back."

- Unknown

Reflection

Integrity isn't just for show. It's most evident in actions performed out of the public eye, reinforcing its genuine and unwavering nature.

Integrity's Role in Legacy

"Wealth consists not in having great possessions, but in having few wants."

- *Epictetus*

Reflection

This Stoic philosopher alludes to the idea that the true wealth of a person is measured not by material possessions, but by their character and integrity.

The Ripple Effects of Integrity

"Live so that when your children think of fairness, caring, and integrity, they think of you."

- *H. Jackson Brown Jr.*

Reflection

Integrity doesn't just impact the individual but also leaves a lasting legacy for future generations, guiding them in their moral compass.

Integrity in Adversity

"The supreme quality for leadership is unquestionably integrity. Without it, no real success is possible."

- *Dwight D. Eisenhower*

Reflection

Eisenhower, having led in times of immense adversity, underlines the pivotal role of integrity. In challenging situations, integrity becomes the beacon guiding toward true success.

Conclusion

Integrity, as seen through the lens of these quotes, is much more than mere honesty. It's a complex value encompassing self-respect, consistency, moral uprightness, and an unwavering commitment to doing right. These quotes aren't just words but profound insights into human character, serving as timeless reminders of the importance of maintaining integrity in all facets of life. By internalizing these reflections, one can strive to lead a life marked by genuine success, peace, and an enduring legacy.

Building and Maintaining Trust in Business

Trust, a seemingly intangible element, forms the bedrock of sustainable and successful business operations. It influences every interaction, from internal employee relations to external customer engagements. While trust is easily broken, rebuilding it can be an arduous task. This detailed exposition provides a comprehensive look into the art and science of building and maintaining trust in the business arena.

Understanding Trust in a Business Context

Defining Trust

At its core, trust in business refers to the confidence stakeholders have in an organization's reliability and integrity.

The Multifaceted Nature of Trust

Trust isn't just about honesty. It encapsulates reliability, competence, and emotional empathy in business operations.

The Importance of Trust in Business

Operational Efficiency

A trusting environment facilitates smoother decision-making processes, reducing the need for extensive oversight.

Enhanced Loyalty

Customers and employees are more loyal to organizations they trust, leading to increased retention and repeat business.

Improved Collaboration

Trust fosters open communication, promoting collaboration among teams and with external partners.

Building Trust with Different Stakeholders

Employees

Transparent communication, consistent recognition, and fair treatment are keys to cultivating trust with the workforce.

Customers

Delivering quality products/services consistently, addressing concerns promptly, and ensuring transparent pricing strategies foster customer trust.

Investors

Financial transparency, regular updates, and ethical business operations are paramount in gaining and retaining investor trust.

Partners

Honesty in commitments, transparent negotiations, and prompt conflict resolution are vital for trust among business partners.

The Pillars of Trust in Business

Reliability

Businesses should deliver consistently, meet their promises, and uphold standards.

Competence

Organizations must demonstrate proficiency and skill in their area of operation, ensuring stakeholders that they are capable.

Intimacy

Showing understanding and care, especially in customer relations, fosters a deeper bond of trust.

Integrity

Adhering to moral and ethical principles is non-negotiable in any trust-building endeavor.

Role of Leadership in Trust-building

Leading by Example

Leaders set the tone for organizational behavior. Their actions, both in success and in adversity, heavily influence the trust climate.

Open Communication

Leaders should be accessible and should communicate openly about challenges, successes, and the way forward.

Accountability

Leaders must own mistakes and take corrective measures, showing that no one is above the organization's values.

Nurturing a Culture of Trust

Transparent Processes

Operations, especially those impacting employees and customers, should be transparent, minimizing feelings of manipulation or deceit.

Feedback Mechanisms

Regular feedback from stakeholders and acting upon it demonstrates that the business values and respects their input.

Consistent Training

Regular training sessions emphasize the importance of trust and impart skills to maintain it.

The Fragility of Trust

The Domino Effect

One breach of trust can cascade, affecting various facets of the business, from employee morale to brand reputation.

The Challenge of Restoration

Rebuilding trust is much harder than building it from scratch, often requiring more resources and time.

Steps to Rebuild Trust

Swift Acknowledgment

Recognize the breach immediately. Denial can further exacerbate mistrust.

Open Communication

Clearly communicate what went wrong, why, and the steps being taken to rectify it.

Restitution Where Possible

If damages have occurred due to the breach, take steps to provide restitution.

Implement Corrective Measures

Ensure that systems, policies, or protocols are in place to prevent future breaches.

Trust in the Digital Age

Data Security

With increasing data breaches, ensuring data privacy and security is paramount to maintain customer trust.

Online Reputation Management

Monitoring and managing online reviews and feedback can greatly influence public trust in a brand.

Trust as an Ongoing Commitment

Regular Reviews

Periodic assessments of trust metrics can help identify potential issues before they escalate.

Evolution with Times

As societal norms and values evolve, businesses should adapt to remain trustworthy in the eyes of their stakeholders.

Conclusion

Trust in business isn't a luxury; it's a necessity. It is the silent currency that drives genuine growth, loyalty, and sustainability. Building and maintaining trust requires continuous effort, self-reflection, and adaptation. In an era where news travels fast and reputation is fragile, businesses can ill afford to be complacent about trust. Prioritizing and nurturing it paves the way for long-lasting success and an enduring legacy in the competitive business landscape.

Chapter 6
Resilience & Overcoming Challenges

In the annals of business history, stories of resilience stand out as beacons of hope, guiding future entrepreneurs and business leaders through the tumultuous seas of the marketplace. Resilience is not just about survival but the ability to thrive and evolve in the face of adversity. This chapter delves deep into the concept of resilience in business, shedding light on its significance and offering guidance on fostering it.

Unpacking Resilience in Business

Definition

Resilience refers to a business's ability to anticipate, prepare for, respond to, and recover from adverse situations, turning challenges into opportunities for growth.

Beyond Mere Recovery

Resilience is not just about bouncing back but bouncing forward, leveraging adversity for innovation and strategic evolution.

The Imperative for Resilience

The Ever-Changing Business Landscape

In a world marked by technological advancements, geopolitical shifts, and evolving consumer behavior, change is the only constant.

The Cost of Complacency

Those businesses that fail to adapt or anticipate challenges often find themselves on the losing end, sometimes facing obsolescence.

Historical Context: Businesses that Embodied Resilience

Apple's Comeback

From near bankruptcy in the late 1990s to becoming a trillion-dollar company, Apple's journey epitomizes resilience and reinvention.

Ford Motor Company

During the 2008 financial crisis, while other automakers sought government bailouts, Ford's foresight and prudent management allowed it to weather the storm on its own terms.

Characteristics of Resilient Businesses

Adaptive Thinking

Rather than rigidly sticking to outdated models, resilient businesses remain flexible, adapting their strategies in response to changing circumstances.

Effective Risk Management

By anticipating potential challenges and having contingencies in place, these businesses minimize the impact of unexpected setbacks.

Strong Organizational Culture

A unified, positive workplace culture fosters collaboration and collective problem-solving during challenging times.

Building Resilience: Strategies and Approaches

Diversification

Avoiding over-reliance on a single revenue stream or market can insulate businesses from sector-specific downturns.

Investing in People

Training and developing employees ensures a skilled workforce capable of navigating through challenges.

Embracing Technology

Leveraging technological tools can enhance efficiency, provide new revenue avenues, and facilitate rapid adaptation.

The Psychological Aspect

Fostering Resilience in Leadership and Teams

Mindset Matters

Leaders should cultivate a growth mindset, viewing challenges as opportunities for learning rather than insurmountable obstacles.

Encouraging Open Communication

Creating an environment where team members feel safe to voice concerns or suggest innovations fosters collective resilience.

Well-being and Mental Health

Recognizing the emotional toll of challenges and offering support, be it through counseling or flexible work arrangements, can boost overall team resilience.

Learning from Failures

The Post-Mortem Analysis

After a setback, dissecting what went wrong, without playing the blame game, offers invaluable insights.

Celebrating the Comebacks

Recognizing and celebrating recovery efforts reinforces the importance of resilience and motivates teams for future challenges.

Resilience in the Face of Global Challenges

Navigating Global Crises

Businesses that demonstrate resilience during global events, such as economic downturns or pandemics, often emerge stronger, gaining market share and enhancing brand reputation.

Sustainability and Long-Term Thinking

Emphasizing sustainable practices not only meets consumer expectations but also prepares businesses for future regulatory and environmental challenges.

The Role of Stakeholder Relationships in Resilience

Loyal Customer Base

Businesses that invest in customer relationships benefit from sustained patronage, even during tough times.

Reliable Supply Chains

Cultivating strong relationships with suppliers ensures continued operations, even when global supply chains face disruptions.

The Future of Resilience: Anticipating the Unpredictable

Scenario Planning

Imagining various future scenarios, even seemingly unlikely ones, and strategizing responses keeps businesses prepared for the unexpected.

Innovation as a Habit

Cultivating a culture of constant innovation ensures businesses remain ahead of the curve, ready to pivot when necessary.

Conclusion

Resilience in business is both an art and a science, a delicate balance between anticipation and reaction. As the business world grows increasingly complex and interdependent, resilience will be the differentiating factor between businesses that merely survive and those that consistently thrive. By understanding its nuances and integrating its principles, businesses can chart a course through challenges, turning potential setbacks into the stepping stones of their success story.

Embracing Setbacks as Learning Opportunities

In the vast tapestry of business evolution, setbacks are inevitable stitches that can either unravel the entire fabric or be woven into a masterpiece. While the natural inclination is to view setbacks negatively, when perceived through the lens of learning, they can catalyze transformational growth. This discourse delves deep into the art of embracing setbacks, converting them from obstacles to invaluable lessons.

The Inevitability of Setbacks

A Universal Experience

From startups to multinational corporations, setbacks are a common thread in the narrative of all businesses.

Nature of Setbacks

They can range from minor operational glitches to major strategic blunders, from internal mistakes to unforeseen external challenges.

The Traditional Perception of Setbacks

The Fear Factor

Many organizational cultures imbue setbacks with a sense of fear, often leading to blame games and avoidance.

The Short-Term Focus

In a world driven by quarterly reports and immediate gratifications, setbacks can be magnified, overshadowing long-term growth prospects.

Reframing the Setback Narrative

The Growth Mindset

Pioneered by psychologist Carol Dweck, this mindset advocates the view that abilities and intelligence can be developed. Setbacks, in this paradigm, are not failures but feedback.

The Power of Perspective

By detaching from immediate emotions and analyzing setbacks objectively, businesses can glean actionable insights.

Benefits of Embracing Setbacks as Learning Opportunities

Innovation Catalyst

The need to address and recover from setbacks can drive businesses to innovate, leading to improved products, services, or processes.

Strengthening the Team

Overcoming challenges collectively can foster unity, resilience, and a shared sense of purpose among team members.

Risk Management

Learning from setbacks enhances a business's ability to anticipate and mitigate future risks.

Strategies to Convert Setbacks into Lessons

Conducting a Post-Mortem

An unbiased analysis of what went wrong, why it went wrong, and how it could have been avoided.

Feedback Loops

Creating channels where employees at all levels can provide feedback ensures diverse perspectives and might uncover overlooked factors.

Adaptive Planning

Using setbacks to inform future strategies, allowing for flexibility and adaptability.

Creating a Culture That Celebrates Learning

Leading from the Front

Leaders must set the tone by owning their mistakes, encouraging transparency, and emphasizing continuous learning.

Rewarding Resilience

Recognizing and celebrating not just successes but also the journey of recovery post-setback can inspire teams.

Training & Development

Regular workshops and training sessions focused on problem-solving, critical thinking, and adaptability.

Real-world Case Studies: Setbacks to Success

Nike's Early Days

Facing bankruptcy, the company reinvented itself, learned from its financial challenges, and emerged stronger, becoming the giant it is today.

SpaceX's Rocket Failures

Elon Musk's aerospace venture witnessed multiple early rocket failures. Yet, learning from each, they have achieved remarkable feats in space transportation.

The Psychological Dynamics: Overcoming the Fear of Setbacks

Emotional Intelligence

Recognizing and regulating the emotions associated with setbacks can lead to clearer decision-making.

The Role of Support Systems

Mentorship, peer groups, and counseling can provide the necessary emotional and strategic support during challenging times.

Long-term Vision: Beyond the Immediate Setback

The Bigger Picture: Instead of fixating on immediate losses, focusing on long-term goals can provide clarity and motivation.

The Evolving Market

Understanding that market dynamics are always in flux can help businesses remain patient and persistent, using setbacks as stepping stones.

Resilience: The Companion of Learning

Interwoven Concepts

Embracing setbacks and resilience go hand in hand. The former provides the lessons, and the latter offers the tenacity to apply them.

Investing in Resilience

Just as businesses invest in R&D, investing in building organizational resilience can yield long-term dividends.

Conclusion

Setbacks, often dreaded and avoided, are in fact hidden treasures of wisdom. They test, refine, and sometimes redefine the mettle of an organization. By embracing them as learning opportunities, businesses not only navigate through their immediate challenges but also fortify themselves for future ones. In the intricate dance of business dynamics, setbacks are not missteps but essential moves, leading to a more synchronized and graceful performance in the market.

Motivational Quotes for Tough Times

Throughout history, words have possessed the power to inspire, uplift, and rejuvenate the human spirit. In challenging times, a few well-chosen words can provide solace, perspective, and the strength to persevere. This exposition delves into a curated list of motivational quotes, unraveling their deeper significance and relevance for individuals navigating through tough times.

The inherent power of words can uplift souls, transform mindsets, and provide solace during turbulent times. Quotes, often brief encapsulations of profound wisdom, have for centuries been a source of guidance and encouragement.

"This too shall pass."

Historical Context

An adage reflecting on the temporary nature of the human condition, it has been used in various forms across different cultures and civilizations.

Relevance

It reminds us of the impermanence of all situations, good or bad. Amidst challenges, it provides hope that difficulties will eventually give way to better times.

"When one door closes, another opens; but we often look so long at the closed door that we do not see the one which has opened for us."

- Alexander Graham Bell

Analysis

This quote speaks to human nature's tendency to ruminate on losses or missed opportunities, often at the expense of recognizing new possibilities.

Application

Especially relevant for those facing rejection or failure, it prompts a shift in perspective to focus on emerging opportunities rather than dwelling on past disappointments.

"It is not the strength of the body that counts, but the strength of the spirit."

- J.R.R. Tolkien

Backdrop

Tolkien, through his vast mythologies, often explored themes of resilience, courage, and the indomitable spirit.

Insight

Physical strength has its limits, but the strength of one's spirit, determination, and will can overcome the gravest of adversities.

"Out of difficulties grow miracles."

- Jean de La Bruyère

Interpretation

Challenges, however overwhelming, can become the fertile ground for unexpected blessings and growth opportunities.

Relevance

For anyone facing setbacks or challenges, this quote serves as a reminder that obstacles can pave the way for transformation and miraculous turnarounds.

"Every adversity, every failure, every heartache carries with it the seed of an equal or greater benefit."

- Napoleon Hill

Analysis

Hill's philosophy revolves around the principle that mindset and perception play pivotal roles in determining outcomes.

Application

In times of loss or failure, seeking lessons and potential benefits can transform adversity into a stepping stone for future success.

"**Success is not final, failure is not fatal: It is the courage to continue that counts.**"

- Winston Churchill

Backdrop

Churchill, having led Britain through its most challenging times, understood the ebbs and flows of success and failure.

Insight

Both success and failure are temporary. What truly matters is the perseverance and determination to keep moving forward regardless of circumstances.

"**When everything seems to be going against you, remember that the airplane takes off against the wind, not with it.**"

- Henry Ford

Analysis

The essence of this quote lies in the recognition that resistance and challenges can be essential catalysts for growth and progress.

Relevance

Particularly significant for entrepreneurs and innovators, it emphasizes the idea that facing challenges head-on can lead to unprecedented heights.

"The only way to achieve the impossible is to believe it is possible."

- Charles Kingsleigh, Alice in Wonderland

Backdrop

A whimsical statement from a fantasy tale, it carries profound wisdom about belief and achieving one's goals.

Application

Essential for dreamers and visionaries, this quote underscores the significance of unwavering belief in one's abilities and ambitions.

"Rock bottom became the solid foundation on which I rebuilt my life."

- J.K. Rowling

Context

Rowling, before her monumental success with the Harry Potter series, faced numerous personal and professional challenges.

Significance

This quote is a testament to the idea that hitting one's lowest point can provide clarity, resolve, and the motivation to rise and rebuild.

"Do not judge me by my successes, judge me by how many times I fell down and got back up again."

- Nelson Mandela

Backdrop

Mandela's life, marked by struggles against apartheid and his subsequent imprisonment, epitomizes resilience.

Relevance

A powerful reminder that the true measure of an individual's strength is not their successes but their ability to rise after falling.

Conclusion

Words, when wielded with wisdom, have the ability to pierce through the gloom, offering light and direction. These quotes, distilled from lifetimes of experiences, offer not just motivation but also profound insights into the nature of challenges, resilience, and the human spirit's indomitable will. In the symphony of life, these words serve as harmonious notes, guiding us through tough times and reminding us of our inherent strength and potential.

Case Studies of Resilience in Business

In the tumultuous world of business, resilience is not just a valuable trait but often a critical determinant of long-term success. Companies that display resilience are able to adapt, transform, and thrive amidst adversity. Let's dive into some iconic case studies that showcase resilience in the face of challenges.

Business landscapes are rife with uncertainties, challenges, and rapid changes. The ability of a company to bounce back from setbacks, adapt, and continue its growth trajectory underscores its resilience. These case studies spotlight companies that displayed remarkable resilience during trying times.

Reinventing to Regain Market Leadership

In the 1990s, Apple faced declining sales, intense competition, and internal strife.

Turning Point

Steve Jobs' return to Apple in 1997 marked the beginning of its transformation. His vision and the introduction of innovative products like the iPod, iPhone, and iPad revolutionized industries.

Outcome

Today, Apple is one of the world's most valuable companies, with a loyal customer base and continued innovation.

Lesson

Visionary leadership and continuous innovation can transform the trajectory of a company, even in dire situations.

Ford Motor Company: Navigating the 2008 Financial Crisis

The 2008 financial crisis hit the auto industry hard. While other major American automakers took government bailouts, Ford chose a different path.

Strategic Moves

Under CEO Alan Mulally, Ford mortgaged all its assets, streamlined its operations, and focused on its core brand.

Outcome

Ford emerged stronger, without government assistance, and reclaimed its position as a leading automaker.

Lesson

Proactive decision-making and belief in core values can empower businesses to navigate through economic downturns without compromising independence.

Netflix:Pivoting from DVDs to Streaming

Founded in 1997, Netflix began as a DVD-by-mail service.

Challenge

As technology evolved, DVD rentals faced potential obsolescence.

Strategic Pivot

Recognizing the shifting dynamics, Netflix introduced streaming services, transforming the entertainment industry.

Outcome

Netflix is now a dominant force in the entertainment world, producing original content and enjoying a massive subscriber base globally.

Lesson

Anticipating industry shifts and being willing to pivot, even if it means disrupting one's own business model, can foster long-term success.

LEGO:Rebuilding a Toy Empire

In the early 2000s, LEGO faced plummeting sales, diversified product confusion, and digital competition.

Revival Strategy

LEGO refocused on its core brick products, engaged with its fan community, and explored strategic partnerships, like its collaboration with the "Harry Potter" and "Star Wars" franchises.

Outcome

By 2017, LEGO reported record-breaking revenues, reaffirming its position as a beloved global brand.

Lesson

Reconnecting with core competencies and leveraging brand loyalists can guide companies back to their essence and success.

Starbucks: Returning to Core Values

In the late 2000s, Starbucks faced saturation, dropping sales, and dilution of its brand experience.

Revival

Howard Schultz, returning as CEO, closed stores for retraining, slowed US expansion, and renewed focus on the customer coffee experience.

Outcome

Starbucks rebounded with enhanced customer loyalty, global expansion, and diversified product offerings.

Lesson

Periodic introspection and re-alignment with foundational values can rejuvenate a brand and restore its market position.

Nintendo: Innovating in the Gaming Industry

Post-2000, Nintendo faced stiff competition from Sony's PlayStation and Microsoft's Xbox.

Innovation

Instead of competing on graphic prowess, Nintendo released the Wii, focusing on gameplay experience and wider audience appeal.

Outcome

The Wii became a monumental success, allowing Nintendo to carve out a unique niche in the gaming industry.

Lesson

Differentiation and understanding target audiences can allow businesses to thrive amidst intense competition.

IBM: From Hardware to Services

Once dominant in the computer hardware industry, IBM faced challenges from newer, more agile competitors in the 1990s.

Transformation

IBM pivoted from primarily selling hardware to offering software and IT services.

Outcome

This transformation into a services company secured IBM's position as a tech powerhouse for the following decades.

Lesson

Companies must be willing to reinvent themselves in the face of industry evolution, leveraging existing strengths in new arenas.

Conclusion

The path to business success is seldom linear. Setbacks, failures, and unexpected challenges are par for the course. However, as these case studies demonstrate, resilience—rooted in foresight, adaptability, and a deep understanding of core values—can guide businesses through storms and toward lasting success. The tales of these companies serve as compelling testaments to the idea that with resilience, businesses can not only survive adversity but emerge stronger and more poised for the future.

Chapter 7
Communication & Influence

In the intricate dance of business, few steps are as vital as the rhythm of communication and the art of influence. Whether it's a CEO setting the strategic direction, a manager motivating a team, or a salesperson courting a potential client, the ability to effectively communicate and persuade is paramount. In this chapter, we will explore the intricacies of these interconnected skills and understand their transformative power in the world of business.

At its core, communication is the act of conveying information, while influence is the ability to shape or affect the behavior and thoughts of others. Together, these twin skills can elevate an organization, fostering understanding, alignment, and action.

The Significance of Effective Communication in Business

Clarity and Understanding

Clear communication ensures all stakeholders have a shared understanding, reducing errors and misinterpretations.

Building Trust

Transparent and open communication fosters trust among team members and stakeholders.

Driving Action

Effective communication empowers teams, providing them with the knowledge and motivation needed to execute tasks efficiently.

Conflict Resolution

Open lines of communication can preempt potential disputes or resolve them more rapidly when they arise.

Components of Effective Communication

Verbal Communication

The spoken word, crucial in meetings, presentations, and daily interactions.

Written Communication

Encompassing emails, reports, and documentation. It requires clarity and precision to avoid ambiguity.

Non-verbal Communication

Body language, tone, and facial expressions, which can often convey more than words.

Listening

A passive but essential component. Active listening involves truly understanding and processing what the other party is communicating.

The Power of Influence in Business

Influence extends beyond mere communication—it's the ability to sway opinions, decisions, and actions.

Building Relationships

The foundation of influence lies in genuine relationships built on trust and mutual respect.

Thought Leadership

By becoming an authority in a specific domain, individuals and organizations can shape industry trends and perceptions.

Negotiation

Effective influencers can drive favorable outcomes in deals, negotiations, and partnerships.

Techniques to Enhance Influence

Storytelling

Sharing narratives that resonate emotionally can drive home a point more effectively than mere data.

Reciprocity

Offering assistance or value often makes others more inclined to help or agree in return.

Consistency and Commitment

People respect and are more likely to be influenced by individuals who are consistent in their words and actions.

Social Proof

Demonstrating that others believe or support an idea can persuade individuals to follow suit.

Communication and Influence in the Digital Age

The rise of digital platforms has transformed how we communicate and influence:

Digital Communication Tools

Platforms like Slack, Zoom, and Microsoft Teams have redefined workplace communication.

Social Media Influence

Brands and individuals wield significant power on platforms like Twitter, LinkedIn, and Instagram, shaping public opinion and trends.

Crisis Communication

In our interconnected world, crises can escalate rapidly. Effective communication is vital to manage and mitigate these situations.

Barriers to Communication and Influence

Cultural Differences

With global businesses, understanding cultural nuances is critical to avoid miscommunication.

Cognitive Biases

People's pre-existing beliefs can distort the reception of information.

Overload of Information

In our information-saturated world, key messages can get lost amidst the noise.

Case Study: Apple's Product Launches

Apple's product launches offer a masterclass in communication and influence.

Setting the Stage

Apple's presentations are meticulously crafted, focusing on the narrative rather than just product specs.

Emotional Resonance

Apple products are positioned not just as gadgets but as tools to "change the world."

Visual Storytelling

Demonstrations and visuals make the product benefits immediately clear and relatable.

Cultivating a Culture of Open Communication

For organizations, fostering a culture where employees feel free to communicate their ideas, concerns, and feedback is vital.

Regular Check-ins

Regular interactions between managers and their teams can keep communication lines open.

Feedback Mechanisms

Tools and platforms where employees can anonymously share feedback can unearth valuable insights.

Conclusion

In the vast theater of business, the acts of communication and influence play starring roles. Mastering these arts is not a luxury but a necessity for individuals and organizations aiming for success. From setting visions to negotiating deals, from resolving conflicts to driving action—the duo of communication and influence underpins every facet of the business world. As the landscape evolves, especially with digital advancements, refining and adapting these skills will remain crucial for future success.

The Art of Effective Communication

In the grand tapestry of human interactions, the threads of communication weave the most intricate patterns. Whether in personal relationships or in the corporate boardroom, effective communication is the cornerstone of understanding, collaboration, and progress. Let's delve deep into this art, exploring its nuances and importance in our interconnected world.

Communication is more than just an exchange of words. It's a complex dance of verbal cues, body language, intentions, emotions, and interpretations. At its best, it leads to clarity, empathy, and action. At its worst, it can result in misunderstanding, conflict, and stagnation.

The Foundations of Effective Communication

Active Listening

This goes beyond just hearing words. It's about understanding the underlying emotions, intentions, and nuances. Active listening involves giving feedback, asking clarifying questions, and showing empathy.

Clarity and Brevity

The best communicators can express complex ideas simply. They avoid jargon, get to the point, and use examples to illustrate their points.

Non-verbal Cues

A significant portion of communication is non-verbal, encompassing gestures, facial expressions, posture, and tone of voice.

Communication in Various Forms

Written Communication

This spans emails, memos, reports, and social media posts. It's essential to consider the audience and use a clear, concise style.

Oral Communication

This covers face-to-face conversations, phone calls, and presentations. Being attentive to feedback, both verbal and non-verbal, is crucial.

Visual Communication

Infographics, diagrams, videos, and presentations fall here. Visual aids can enhance understanding, especially for complex topics.

Barriers to Effective Communication

Understanding the challenges in communication is the first step to overcoming them.

Cultural Differences

In a globalized world, understanding and respecting cultural nuances in communication styles is crucial.

Cognitive Biases

Pre-existing beliefs can distort how messages are received and interpreted.

Environmental Distractions

Physical noise, digital distractions, or even mental preoccupations can hinder effective communication.

The Emotional Dimension of Communication

Empathy

Stepping into someone else's shoes can enhance understanding and rapport. It allows for better anticipation of reactions and tailoring of messages.

Emotional Intelligence (EQ)

This is the ability to recognize, understand, and manage our own emotions while recognizing and influencing the emotions of others. High EQ individuals navigate conversations with greater tact and effectiveness.

Feedback: The Mirror to Communication

Feedback provides a reflection of how messages are received and understood.

Constructive Feedback

Rather than mere criticism, this aims to help the recipient grow. It's specific, objective, and ideally, actionable.

Receiving Feedback

This is as much an art as giving it. It requires an open mind, devoid of defensiveness, and the ability to sift through comments for valuable insights.

Digital Age: The Evolution and Challenges of Communication

With the proliferation of digital tools, communication methods have expanded but so have the challenges.

Overcommunication

The ease of sending messages can sometimes lead to information overload.

Loss of Personal Touch

Texts and emails lack non-verbal cues, leading to potential misunderstandings.

Speed vs. Quality

The immediacy of digital communication tools can sometimes prioritize speed over thoughtful, quality interactions.

Strategies for Effective Communication

Know Your Audience

Tailoring your message to the audience's level of understanding, interests, and needs can make it more impactful.

Structure Your Message

A clear beginning, middle, and end, with signposts along the way, can guide your audience through your message.

Practice Active Listening

This not only shows respect but also ensures that you fully understand the other person's perspective.

Seek Feedback

Regularly ask for feedback to refine your communication style and ensure your messages hit the mark.

Case Study: The 'Open Door' Policy of Successful Leaders

Many successful organizations have leaders who adopt an 'open door' policy, promoting direct communication across all levels. This approach:

Encourages Transparency

Employees feel they can raise concerns without layers of bureaucracy.

Fosters Trust

Leaders become more approachable, leading to increased trust and loyalty.

Enhances Decision-making

Direct feedback can lead to more informed decisions.

Conclusion

Mastering the art of effective communication is a lifelong journey. In a world brimming with noise, being able to convey thoughts, intentions, and emotions clearly is a skill of immeasurable value. Beyond the workplace, it enriches personal relationships and societal interactions. As the tools and platforms of communication evolve, the core principles remain timeless: understanding, clarity, empathy, and feedback. Embracing these pillars can unlock not only personal and professional growth but also pave the way for collaborative progress in our interconnected world.

Powerful Quotes on Influence

Influence is an intangible yet potent force that can inspire change, shape perceptions, and drive actions. Through the ages, thought leaders, philosophers, and influencers have reflected on its power, leaving behind nuggets of wisdom. Here, we'll explore some of these impactful quotes on influence and delve deep into their underlying messages and implications.

Influence, in its purest form, is the ability to affect the character, development, or behavior of someone or something without exerting overt force. Whether it's a leader inspiring a nation, a teacher molding young minds, or a parent guiding a child, influence is at work. The chosen quotes in this exploration provide insights into the multifaceted nature of influence.

"Leadership is not about being in charge. It is about taking care of those in your charge."

– Simon Sinek

Explanation

True leadership is not about wielding authority, but rather about stewardship—taking responsibility for and serving those you lead. Influence here is subtle, built on trust and mutual respect.

"The key to successful leadership today is influence, not authority."

– Ken Blanchard

Explanation

In today's interconnected, collaborative world, traditional hierarchies are often less effective than persuasive abilities. Leaders who can inspire and influence gain more genuine followership than those who rely merely on positional power.

"People don't buy what you do; they buy why you do it."

– Simon Sinek

Explanation

Authenticity is a significant influencer. People are more likely to be influenced or buy into an idea or product when they believe in the 'why' behind it—the purpose or passion driving it.

"To influence people, don't talk about your own achievements. Instead, talk about theirs."

– Dan Reiland

Explanation

One of the most effective ways to influence others is to make them feel seen and valued. Recognizing and celebrating others' achievements can build rapport and open avenues for positive influence.

"The highest of distinctions is service to others."

– King George VI

Explanation

True influence isn't about elevating oneself, but lifting others up. Service to others is a profound way to leave a lasting impact and legacy.

"You don't have to be a person of influence to be influential. In fact, the most influential people in my life are probably not even aware of the things they've taught me."

– Scott Adams

Explanation

Influence isn't always tied to fame or stature. Everyday interactions, simple gestures, or shared wisdom can leave indelible marks. The unsung heroes in our lives—the mentors, family, or friends—often wield the most genuine influence.

"The art of communication is the language of leadership."

– James Humes

Explanation

Effective communication is foundational to influence. Being able to articulate ideas, evoke emotions, and inspire action is the hallmark of influential leadership.

"Influence is our inner ability to lift people up to our perspectives."

– Joseph Wong

Explanation

At its core, influence is about perspective-sharing. It's the skill of bringing people on board, letting them see through your lens, and guiding them towards a shared vision or understanding.

"Example is not the main thing in influencing others. It is the only thing."

– Albert Schweitzer

Explanation

Actions speak louder than words. The most persuasive form of influence is leading by example. What we do, how we behave, and the values we embody exert a more profound influence than mere words.

Case Study: Mahatma Gandhi's Influence

Mahatma Gandhi once said, "Be the change that you wish to see in the world."

Explanation

Gandhi's life was a testament to the power of influence through action. He led India's freedom struggle not through force, but through non-violence, inspiring millions. His beliefs, actions, and the sacrifices he made for his principles showcased how one could influence vast multitudes without authority or force, but with integrity and purpose.

Conclusion

The realm of influence is vast and profound. It reminds us that every interaction is an opportunity to leave an imprint, to guide, and to inspire. The quotes explored here, while only a fraction of the wisdom on influence, provide a roadmap to understanding its depth and potential. Whether we're leaders, educators, parents, or friends, the art of influence is a tool we can hone and wield for collective growth, understanding, and progress.

Crafting Messages That Resonate

Communication is an age-old tool, yet its potency lies in how it's wielded. In a world saturated with messages, how do you ensure yours stands out? How do you craft a message that doesn't just get heard but truly resonates? This exploration delves into the nuances of creating impactful, memorable messages.

In the vast ocean of messages, from billboards to tweets, creating a message that sticks is akin to finding a needle in a haystack. But it's not about volume; it's about value. A resonant message touches hearts, changes minds, and spurs actions. But how is such a message crafted?

Understanding the Audience

Before crafting a message, one must understand its recipients.

Demographics

Age, gender, education, and other basic factors can shape how a message is received.

Psychographics

Dive deeper. Understand your audience's values, aspirations, fears, and motivations.

Feedback Mechanisms

Employ surveys, focus groups, or direct interactions to get insights into your audience's minds.

The Power of Authenticity

Genuine messages resonate because they're grounded in truth.

Transparency

Honesty builds trust, making your message more impactful.

Relatability

Sharing personal stories or vulnerabilities makes the message more human and relatable.

Clarity and Simplicity

In a world of information overload, less can indeed be more.

Avoid Jargon

Use simple language that's universally understood.

Structured Communication

Clear beginnings, middles, and ends guide the audience through your message.

Emotional Connectivity

Emotions drive actions. Tap into them.

Storytelling

Narratives captivate human minds. Frame your message within a compelling story.

Visual Aids

Images, infographics, or videos can evoke emotions more potently than words alone.

Consistency is Key

A message heard once is easily forgotten; repeated, it sticks.

Reiteration

Repetition, without being redundant, reinforces the message.

Consistent Values

Ensure the core values driving your messages remain steady.

Tailoring to the Medium

Different platforms necessitate different message treatments.

Social Media

Short, snappy, and shareable content wins.

Long-form Articles

Dive deep, providing detailed insights and value.

Video

Engage both visually and audibly, ensuring your message is compelling on both fronts.

Invoking a Call to Action (CTA)

A resonant message often compels its audience to act.

Clear CTAs

Specify what you want your audience to do next.

Motivation

Provide a reason or benefit for the suggested action.

The Role of Feedback

Every message sent out can be refined based on its reception.

Listen Actively

Be open to criticism and praise alike.

Iterate

Use feedback to craft even more resonant messages in the future.

Case StudyApple's "Think Different" Campaign

Apple's iconic campaign is a masterclass in crafting resonant messages.

Challenging the Status Quo

The campaign invoked a spirit of rebellion, resonating with innovators and creatives.

Emotional Appeal

By showcasing iconic personalities, the campaign linked Apple's brand to the pantheon of world-changers.

Simplicity and Clarity

The phrase "Think Different" is succinct, yet powerful.

Potential Pitfalls in Message Crafting

Overloading Information

Avoid overwhelming your audience.

Being Inauthentic

Messages that seem fake or manufactured can repel rather than attract.

Neglecting Feedback

Ignoring audience feedback can make subsequent messages fall flat.

Conclusion

Crafting a message that truly resonates is both an art and a science. It demands an understanding of one's audience, authenticity, clarity, and emotional depth. In the cacophony of today's digital age, a resonant message is not just one that's heard, but one that lingers, provoking thought and inspiring action. As communicators, the challenge is not just to speak, but to be truly understood, remembered, and to leave a lasting impact.

Chapter 8
Growth & Continuous Learning

In the dynamic world of business, the principle of stagnation versus growth determines an organization's life span and an individual's career trajectory. While growth is often visualized in terms of numbers and profits, its most sustainable form arises from a culture of continuous learning. This chapter delves into why continuous learning is the bedrock of genuine growth and how businesses and individuals can cultivate it.

The only constant in life is change. In the realms of business and personal development, this change is channeled most productively through continuous learning. But what does continuous learning entail, and why is it so intricately linked with growth?

The Paradigm of Continuous Learning

Continuous learning refers to the persistent and voluntary act of acquiring new knowledge or skills, irrespective of one's age or professional standing.

Beyond Formal Education

While traditional education lays a foundation, continuous learning builds the house, filling gaps and adapting to evolving scenarios.

The Business Case for Continuous Learning

Adapting to Market Changes

In fluctuating markets, organizations armed with the latest knowledge and skills can pivot effectively.

Innovation

Continuous learning breeds innovation by introducing new perspectives and techniques.

Employee Retention

A culture of learning attracts and retains top talent, as employees value personal and professional growth.

Continuous Learning for Individuals

Career Advancement

Individuals who prioritize learning are more likely to climb the career ladder, equipped to handle diverse roles and responsibilities.

Personal Fulfillment

Beyond professional benefits, continuous learning caters to intellectual curiosity and personal satisfaction.

Building Resilience

Continual learners are better equipped to handle setbacks, having a broader skill set and knowledge base to fall back on.

Cultivating a Learning Culture in Organizations

Training and Workshops

Regularly updating employees' skills ensures they remain at the forefront of industry developments.

Encourage Knowledge Sharing

Platforms like in-house seminars or knowledge-sharing sessions can democratize learning.

Reward Learning

Recognize and incentivize employees who prioritize and apply new knowledge.

Tools for Continuous Learning

Online Platforms

Websites like Coursera, Udemy, and Khan Academy provide courses on a plethora of topics.

Reading

Books, journals, and articles remain invaluable resources.

Networking

Interacting with peers, attending seminars, or joining clubs can open doors to new knowledge and perspectives.

Challenges in Promoting Continuous Learning

Resistance to Change

Both individuals and organizations can fall into the comfort zone trap, avoiding the unfamiliar.

Overwhelm

The sheer volume of available information can paralyze rather than inspire.

Lack of Clear ROI

The benefits of continuous learning might not be immediately tangible, leading to skepticism.

Case Study: Microsoft's Growth Mindset

Under Satya Nadella's leadership, Microsoft shifted from a "know-it-all" to a "learn-it-all" culture.

Background

Recognizing stagnation, Nadella sought to reinvigorate Microsoft's culture.

Implementation

Employees were encouraged to embrace risks, learn from failures, and prioritize learning.

Outcome

Microsoft witnessed a resurgence in innovation, employee satisfaction, and market relevance.

The Future of Continuous Learning

AI and Personalized Learning

AI-driven platforms can curate personalized learning paths, optimizing content based on individual needs and progress.

Lifelong Learning

As the traditional career model evolves, lifelong learning might become the norm, with individuals continually adapting to new roles and industries.

Conclusion

Growth, in its most profound sense, is an inward journey as much as an outward expansion. In the rapidly evolving landscapes of industries, economies, and personal career paths, continuous learning remains the beacon guiding this growth. It's not just about acquiring information but internalizing knowledge, applying it innovatively, and creating value for oneself and the larger community. As the boundaries of what we know continually expand, the commitment to learning ensures that we grow alongside, if not ahead of, the curve.

The Journey of Self-Improvement

Embarking on the path of self-improvement is a decision that seeks to harness one's potential and broaden horizons. More than a series of actions, it's a mindset, a continuous pursuit. Here, we explore the facets of self-improvement, its significance, methods, and challenges, and how it intertwines with every aspect of human life.

Self-improvement is the deliberate and purposeful act of enhancing one's skills, knowledge, character, and overall quality of life. It is the quest to become the best version of oneself. But what drives this urge, and how does one embark on such a journey?

The Inherent Desire for Betterment

Every individual, deep down, harbors a desire to better oneself. This drive stems from:

Evolutionary Perspectives

Our ancestors' need to adapt and improve for survival has trickled down through generations.

Personal Satisfaction

Growth and progress offer intrinsic rewards, creating feelings of fulfillment and contentment.

Areas of Self-Improvement

While the scope is vast, some universal areas include:

Mental Growth

Enhancing knowledge, critical thinking, and problem-solving.

Emotional Growth

Cultivating emotional intelligence, empathy, and resilience.

Physical Growth

Focusing on health, fitness, and well-being.

Spiritual Growth

Exploring purpose, beliefs, and connection with the universe.

Why Embark on This Journey?

The quest for self-improvement offers myriad benefits:

Boosted Self-Esteem

Personal growth directly correlates with self-worth and confidence.

Better Relationships

Enhanced emotional intelligence fosters understanding and harmony in relationships.

Career Progression

Acquiring new skills and knowledge can catalyze professional growth.

Enhanced Quality of Life

Overall well-being improves, leading to a richer life experience.

Tools for Self-Improvement

The journey is unique for everyone, but certain tools can guide the process:

Books

Timeless sources of wisdom, offering insights into various facets of life.

Online Platforms

Websites, courses, and webinars cater to diverse learning needs.

Mentors and Coaches

Personalized guidance can expedite growth.

Meditation and Mindfulness

Tools to introspect, understand oneself, and stay present.

Setting Realistic Goals

It's vital to set achievable targets

S.M.A.R.T Goals

Specific, Measurable, Achievable, Relevant, and Time-bound objectives provide a clear roadmap.

Visualizing Success

Imagining the end goal can be a potent motivator.

Regular Review

Periodically assessing progress ensures alignment with goals.

The Role of Habits

Power of Consistency

Regular, small actions culminate in substantial growth.

Cultivating Positive Habits

Disciplines like reading daily or regular exercise can be transformative.

Overcoming Negative Patterns

Recognizing and addressing detrimental habits is equally crucial.

Embracing Failures

Missteps are an integral part of the journey:

Lessons in Disguise

Every setback offers a lesson, an opportunity to grow.

Cultivating Resilience

Bouncing back from failures builds emotional strength.

Reframing Mindset

Viewing challenges as growth opportunities shifts the perspective.

Challenges in the Journey

While rewarding, the path isn't devoid of obstacles:

Resistance to Change

Stepping out of comfort zones can be daunting.

Information Overload

The plethora of resources can be overwhelming.

External Naysayers

Facing skepticism or discouragement from others.

Continuous Evolution

Self-improvement isn't a destination but an ongoing journey:

Lifelong Learning

The quest for knowledge never truly ends.

Adapting to Life's Phases

Different life stages will present new challenges and growth areas.

Giving Back

As one grows, there's an opportunity to mentor and guide others.

Conclusion

The journey of self-improvement is as ancient as humanity itself. It's a testament to the human spirit's indomitable will to evolve, adapt, and thrive. From ancient philosophers to modern-day thinkers, the quest for growth remains a universal pursuit. Whether driven by personal aspirations, professional ambitions, or a simple love for learning, self-improvement enriches life in myriad ways. As individuals, our commitment to this journey not only enhances our own lives but also contributes to the world, making it a better place, one step at a time.

Quotes on the Importance of Learning: A Deep Dive into Lifelong Education

"Live as if you were to die tomorrow. Learn as if you were to live forever."

- Mahatma Gandhi

The human quest for knowledge is as ancient as our existence. Through the ages, scholars, leaders, and thinkers have emphasized the importance of learning, not just as a means to an end but as an end in itself. Let's explore the profound insights from various quotes on the value of learning.

The Eternal Flame of Curiosity

"The important thing is not to stop questioning. Curiosity has its own reason for existing."

- Albert Einstein

Explanation

Einstein suggests that curiosity isn't just a means to find answers but is valuable in itself. The very act of questioning, of being curious, is intrinsic to human nature and drives us towards understanding and knowledge.

Learning as a Lifelong Journey

"Education is the kindling of a flame, not the filling of a vessel."

- Socrates

Explanation

Socrates highlights that education isn't about rote memorization or simply filling one's mind with facts. Instead, it's about igniting a passion, a curiosity that drives an individual to continually seek knowledge throughout their life.

The Power of Continuous Growth

"Anyone who stops learning is old, whether at twenty or eighty. Anyone who keeps learning stays young."

- *Henry Ford*

Explanation

Ford emphasizes that age isn't merely a factor of years but of mindset. The act of learning keeps one's mind agile and youthful, regardless of physical age.

The Interconnectedness of Knowledge

"The more I read, the more I acquire, the more certain I am that I know nothing."

- *Voltaire*

Explanation

As one delves deeper into the vast ocean of knowledge, it becomes evident how much there still is to know. This humbling realization is a testament to the interconnectedness and boundlessness of knowledge.

Learning Beyond Classrooms

"I have never let my schooling interfere with my education."

- *Mark Twain*

Explanation

Twain draws a distinction between formal schooling and genuine education. While structured education has its value, real learning often occurs outside traditional classrooms, through experiences, interactions, and introspection.

The Value of Diverse Knowledge

"It is the mark of an educated mind to be able to entertain a thought without accepting it."

- Aristotle

Explanation

Aristotle suggests that true education equips one with the ability to consider diverse perspectives and ideas, even those that might not align with one's own beliefs, without necessarily adopting them.

The Role of Mistakes in Learning

"Mistakes are the portals of discovery."

- James Joyce

Explanation

Joyce reminds us that errors aren't failures but opportunities. Every mistake offers a chance to learn, to discover something new, making them invaluable in the learning process.

Self-Empowerment Through Knowledge

"Knowledge makes a man unfit to be a slave."

- Frederick Douglass

Explanation

Douglass, an escaped slave turned abolitionist, emphasizes the empowering nature of knowledge. Being educated, being aware, grants an individual the ability to resist oppression and seek freedom.

Learning as an Antidote to Boredom

"The cure for boredom is curiosity. There is no cure for curiosity."

- *Dorothy Parker*

Explanation

Parker implies that a curious mind, always eager to learn, will never encounter boredom. Such a mind constantly seeks out new knowledge, experiences, and adventures.

The Humbling Nature of Learning

"The more you know, the more you realize you don't know."

- *Aristotle*

Explanation

As echoed by Voltaire, Aristotle points out that with every new piece of knowledge acquired, one becomes more aware of the vast unknown. It's a humbling journey that underscores the infinite nature of learning.

Conclusion

Through the lens of these quotes, we glean the multifaceted nature of learning. From fostering a youthful spirit to enabling empowerment, from igniting passion to encouraging humility, the act of learning transcends the mere acquisition of facts. It shapes characters, molds societies, and, most importantly, defines what it means to be human. As we navigate the vast expanse of existence, these quotes serve as beacons, reminding us of the invaluable treasure that is knowledge and the never-ending journey of learning.

Strategies for Personal and Professional Growth

The journey of personal and professional growth is continuous, demanding, and deeply rewarding. It is a path punctuated by successes, failures, learnings, and transformations. To navigate this journey effectively, one must arm oneself with a set of strategies that can guide actions and decisions. These strategies serve as a roadmap, leading individuals to achieve their fullest potential.

Setting Clear Objectives

Objective is the first step towards clarity in pursuit.

Why It Matters

Without a clear objective, efforts can become scattered, leading to reduced efficacy in achieving goals.

Implementation Strategy

Use the S.M.A.R.T (Specific, Measurable, Achievable, Relevant, Time-bound) criteria to define objectives. This ensures that goals are not only well-defined but also actionable.

Continuous Learning

Knowledge is endless, and so should be the pursuit.

Why It Matters

he world is constantly evolving, with new technologies, methodologies, and practices emerging regularly.

Implementation Strategy

Dedicate time to read books, attend workshops, enroll in courses, or listen to podcasts. Embrace a growth mindset and recognize that learning is a lifelong endeavor.

Seeking Feedback

Growth thrives in the reflection of others.

Why It Matters

Feedback offers a mirror to one's actions and decisions, highlighting areas of improvement.

Implementation Strategy

Regularly ask peers, supervisors, or mentors for feedback. More importantly, be open to receiving it and act upon constructive critiques.

Networking

Connections open doors to opportunities and wisdom.

Why It Matters

Building professional relationships can offer new perspectives, opportunities, and insights that might not be accessible otherwise.

Implementation Strategy

Attend industry conferences, join professional organizations, or participate in webinars. Engage actively on professional platforms like LinkedIn.

Time Management

Time, when harnessed, becomes an ally in growth.

Why It Matters

Effective time management ensures optimal productivity and offers the space to pursue growth opportunities.

Implementation Strategy

Use tools like calendars, to-do lists, or time-tracking apps. Allocate specific blocks of time for different tasks and adhere to them.

Embracing Failures

Mistakes are the stepping stones of progress.

Why It Matters

Failures, though disheartening, offer invaluable lessons.

Implementation Strategy

When faced with setbacks, analyze what went wrong, learn from the mistakes, and iterate upon the approach.

Prioritizing Mental and Physical Well-being

A sound mind and body are the pillars of sustained growth.

Why It Matters

Personal and professional growth demands a lot, both mentally and physically. Maintaining good health ensures one is equipped to handle these demands.

Implementation Strategy

Incorporate regular exercise into your routine, prioritize sleep, meditate, and ensure a balanced diet. Take breaks when needed.

Embracing Adaptability

Change is constant; adaptability is the key.

Why It Matters

An adaptable individual can navigate the ever-changing landscapes of personal and professional terrains with ease.

Implementation Strategy

Stay informed about industry trends, be open to changing long-held beliefs, and be willing to step out of comfort zones.

Seeking Mentorship

Guidance illuminates the path of growth.

Why It Matters

Mentors offer insights drawn from their experiences, helping mentees avoid common pitfalls and capitalize on opportunities.

Implementation Strategy

Identify industry leaders or senior professionals and approach them for mentorship. Engage in meaningful discussions and seek their counsel on pivotal decisions.

Investing in Soft Skills

Beyond technical know-how, soft skills weave the fabric of professional success.

Why It Matters

Communication, teamwork, empathy, and other soft skills determine how one collaborates, leads, and contributes to an organization.

Implementation Strategy

Attend workshops focused on enhancing soft skills, practice active listening, and engage in group activities to foster teamwork.

Conclusion

Personal and professional growth is a multifaceted journey, with each strategy representing a piece of the larger puzzle. While every individual's path is unique, these strategies offer a foundational framework upon which bespoke growth plans can be built. Whether you're at the onset of your career, in the middle, or in leadership positions, integrating these strategies can steer you towards profound growth, success, and fulfillment. As the adage goes, "Growth and comfort do not coexist." Embrace the discomfort, challenges, and uncertainties, for they are the harbingers of unparalleled growth.

Chapter 9
Work-Life Balance & Self-Care

In today's fast-paced world, striking a balance between work demands and personal life has become a crucial challenge. The quest for success often overshadows the importance of self-care and personal well-being. This chapter delves into the significance of work-life balance and self-care, offering insights and strategies to navigate this essential equilibrium.

The Essence of Work-Life Balance

Defining the Thin Line Between Commitment and Overcommitment.

Why It Matters

Achieving work-life balance ensures both professional success and personal well-being, preventing burnout and ensuring longevity in one's career.

Insights

A true balance doesn't always mean an equal division of time but rather an equitable division of energy and focus.

The Repercussions of Imbalance

The Tipping Point: When Work Takes Over.

Why It Matters

Continuous neglect of personal life or health can lead to stress, health issues, relationship strains, and reduced productivity.

Insights

Burnout is a real and pressing issue, with tangible repercussions on mental health and overall life satisfaction.

Recognizing the Signs

The Red Flags of a Disproportioned Life.

Why It Matters

Early recognition of imbalance can lead to timely interventions, preventing long-term adverse effects.

Insights

Constant fatigue, irritability, reduced performance, sleep disturbances, and a feeling of detachment are telltale signs of a skewed work-life balance.

Strategies for Achieving Balance

Creating Harmony in the Midst of Chaos.

Why It Matters

Proactive strategies can help in achieving and maintaining a harmonious balance between work and personal life.

Implementation Strategies:

Set clear boundaries

Disconnect from work during off-hours.

Prioritize tasks

Not everything that is urgent is important.

Time management

Allocate specific times for work, relaxation, and personal pursuits.

Take breaks

Short, regular breaks can boost productivity and mental well-being.

The Role of Employers in Promoting Balance

From Rhetoric to Reality:Making Work-Life Balance a Corporate Culture.

Why It Matters

Organizations play a pivotal role in promoting a culture that values balance.

Insights

Companies with policies that promote work-life balance often see reduced employee turnover, higher job satisfaction, and improved productivity.

The Art of Self-Care

Beyond Balance: Prioritizing Self in the Grind of Life.

Why It Matters

Self-care is an essential component of mental health, emotional well-being, and overall life satisfaction.

Implementation Strategies

Physical self-care: Regular exercise, a balanced diet, and adequate sleep.

Emotional self-care

Engage in activities that bring joy, maintain close personal relationships, and seek therapy if needed.

Spiritual self-care

Meditation, mindfulness practices, or connecting with nature.

Setting Boundaries

Drawing the Line for Personal Peace.

Why It Matters

Boundaries ensure that one's personal space, time, and energy aren't constantly infringed upon.

Insights

The ability to say "no" is empowering. It protects mental and emotional well-being while ensuring that one isn't stretched too thin.

The Role of Technology

Boon or Bane: The Digital Impact on Work-Life Balance.

Why It Matters

In the digital age, technology can either facilitate balance or exacerbate imbalance, depending on its use.

Insights

While technology has blurred the lines between work and personal life, it also offers tools like digital calendars, productivity apps, and wellness trackers to promote balance.

The Global Perspective

Work-Life Balance Across Cultures: A Comparative Analysis.

Why It Matters

Different cultures have varied approaches to work-life balance, and understanding these can offer fresh perspectives.

Insights

Countries like Denmark and Finland are often ranked high in work-life balance due to factors like shorter work weeks, ample vacation time, and societal emphasis on personal well-being.

Preparing for the Future

The Evolving Nature of Work and the Quest for Balance.

Why It Matters

The nature of work is continually evolving, with remote work, gig economy, and flexible hours becoming the norm. Adapting to these changes is crucial for future balance.

Insights

Embracing change, continuous learning, and flexibility are key to maintaining work-life balance in the future landscape of work.

Conclusion

Work-Life Balance and Self-Care aren't mere buzzwords but essential components of a fulfilling life. Achieving this balance isn't a one-time act but a continuous process of introspection, adjustment, and alignment. As the boundaries between work and personal life become increasingly porous, the emphasis on preserving this equilibrium becomes paramount. After all, at the heart of professional success lies personal well-being, and in the pursuit of achievements, the self should never be sidelined.

Nurturing the Self in a Busy World

In the age of ever-present technology, the relentless pace of modern life, and a world that seemingly never sleeps, finding time to nurture oneself can seem like a daunting task. The imperative of the modern age is often one of "doing" rather than "being", leading many to feel overwhelmed, burned out, and detached from their inner selves. But it's precisely in these chaotic times that the need to nurture oneself becomes paramount.

The Modern Predicament

Today's world is characterized by an abundance of opportunities and the simultaneous challenge of endless distractions. The push for productivity, coupled with the weight of societal expectations, has taken a toll on individual well-being. The ceaseless cycle of meetings, deadlines, and digital notifications makes it difficult to find moments of stillness.

But, what does this perpetual busyness cost us? Research suggests that a constant state of "busyness" can lead to chronic stress, reduced creativity, and a diminished sense of self-worth. It's no wonder that mental health issues are on the rise in many parts of the world.

The Importance of Nurturing the Self

Nurturing the self is more than just a form of self-care; it's a deep commitment to understanding, valuing, and caring for one's innermost needs and desires. It's about recognizing one's worth outside of societal expectations and achievements.

- Benefits of nurturing the self include:
- Enhanced mental and emotional well-being.
- Improved resilience to life's challenges.
- A deeper sense of purpose and direction.
- Strengthened relationships with others due to a better relationship with oneself.

Strategies for Nurturing the Self

Mindfulness and Meditation: In a world filled with external noise, mindfulness offers an oasis of inner calm. Practices like meditation, deep breathing, and journaling can help individuals connect with their inner selves, fostering a sense of peace and clarity.

Digital Detox

Periodic breaks from technology, especially social media, can alleviate feelings of comparison, anxiety, and information overload. Designating tech-free times or zones in one's daily routine can be remarkably liberating.

Engage in Creative Expression

Whether it's painting, writing, dancing, or any form of art, creative expression is a powerful tool for self-exploration and healing. It allows for the processing of emotions and fosters a sense of accomplishment.

Prioritize Physical Well-being

The mind and body are deeply interconnected. Regular exercise, a balanced diet, and adequate sleep are foundational to nurturing oneself.

Reconnect with Nature

Nature has a profound healing effect. Taking walks in a park, gardening, or even just sitting under the sky can offer a deep sense of connection and tranquility.

The Role of Boundaries

Setting boundaries isn't about isolation but about preservation. It's crucial to recognize one's limits and communicate them clearly. Whether it's declining an additional work assignment or choosing to spend a weekend in solitude, setting boundaries ensures that one's energy and well-being aren't constantly depleted.

Building a Support System

No one nurtures themselves in isolation. Building a support system of friends, family, or professionals who understand and respect one's need for self-care is essential. This network serves as a reminder to prioritize oneself, offering encouragement and support during challenging times.

Continuous Learning and Growth

Nurturing the self also involves personal growth. This can be achieved through reading, attending workshops, or simply engaging in new experiences. Expanding one's horizons enriches the soul and offers fresh perspectives on life.

The Challenge of Self-compassion

In a world that often emphasizes perfection, it's easy to be one's harshest critic. However, self-compassion involves treating oneself with the same kindness and understanding as one would treat a dear friend. It's about acknowledging that everyone, including oneself, is a work in progress.

Rituals and Routines

Establishing daily rituals, no matter how small, can anchor one's day and provide moments of solace. This could be as simple as having a cup of tea in silence, reading a few pages of a book, or practicing gratitude.

Conclusion: Making Peace with Oneself

In the relentless chase of accomplishments, it's easy to lose oneself. However, the journey of nurturing the self is a profound act of rebellion in today's world. It's a declaration that one's worth isn't determined solely by achievements or societal standards. By committing to nurture oneself, individuals can reclaim their peace, purpose, and joy, making life not just a series of tasks but a rich tapestry of experiences.

In the end, nurturing oneself isn't a luxury; it's a necessity. For in the words of Lao Tzu, "Knowing others is wisdom, knowing yourself is Enlightenment."

Quotes on Balance and Well-being

The art of balancing one's life and maintaining well-being is as old as humanity itself. Through the ages, philosophers, poets, leaders, and thinkers have contemplated and shared their wisdom on the subject. In this chapter, we will delve deep into some of the most poignant quotes that highlight the importance of balance and well-being, understanding their context, and interpreting their relevance in today's fast-paced world.

"Happiness is not a matter of intensity but of balance, order, rhythm, and harmony."

Thomas Merton

This quote by Thomas Merton, a Trappist monk known for his deep insights into spirituality and life's purpose, underscores the misconception of equating happiness with extreme emotions or experiences. True happiness, he suggests, is achieved through a stable equilibrium in life. Just as a musical piece needs rhythm and harmony, our lives require a balance between work and rest, socializing and solitude, challenges and relaxation. In our pursuit of heightened experiences, we often overlook the simple, rhythmic joys that bring genuine contentment.

"**Life is like riding a bicycle. To keep your balance, you must keep moving.**"

Albert Einstein

Einstein's analogy perfectly captures the essence of life's journey. Balance doesn't mean stagnation; it's about moving forward, even when challenges arise. Just as a stationary bicycle is likely to tip over, staying stuck or dwelling on past hardships can disrupt our life's equilibrium. The key is to learn, adapt, and persistently move forward, maintaining our balance through action.

"**The best and safest thing is to keep a balance in your life, acknowledge the great powers around us and in us. If you can do that, and live that way, you are really a wise man.**"

Euripides

Ancient Greek playwright Euripides highlights the interplay of external and internal forces in our lives. Recognizing the immense powers (both challenges and opportunities) around us and the inherent strengths within us can lead to a centered existence. This self-awareness and external acknowledgment foster resilience, humility, and balance, essential attributes for a fulfilling life.

"**It's all about quality of life and finding a happy balance between work and friends and family.**"

Philip Green

The British business magnate emphasizes the golden triad of life: work, friends, and family. While professional achievements can be immensely satisfying, it's the shared moments with loved ones that truly enrich our lives. Creating a synergy between these spheres, rather than letting one overshadow the others, ensures a holistic sense of well-being.

"To be calm is the highest achievement of the self."

Zen Proverb

In the Zen tradition, calmness isn't just an emotion but a profound state of being. Amidst the storms of life's challenges, personal conflicts, and societal pressures, retaining one's inner calm is a testament to self-mastery. Achieving this tranquility requires introspection, self-awareness, and often, a deliberate disengagement from external chaos.

"Balance is not something you find, it's something you create."

Jana Kingsford

Kingsford's words are a reminder that balance isn't a passive state awaiting discovery but an active endeavor. It's about making conscious choices, setting priorities, and sometimes, making tough decisions to ensure our physical, emotional, and spiritual well-being.

"Well-being is not about always being safe or fed or comfortable. Rather, it is learning to walk the line between the two, to balance, to move back-and-forth or back-and-forth between challenge and safety, like kids on a playground who climb to ever higher heights and then jump, catching the breath at the last moment, swinging into the air."

Peggy O'Mara

O'Mara's analogy of children on a playground paints a vivid picture of well-being. True well-being doesn't mean perpetual comfort. It's about pushing boundaries, taking risks, and reveling in the exhilarating moments of life while also ensuring our safety nets. This dynamic interplay keeps life vibrant and meaningful.

"Do not let the behavior of others destroy your inner peace."

Dalai Lama

The spiritual leader of Tibet offers profound advice about preserving one's inner sanctum. While we cannot control external circumstances or people's actions, we have the power to control our reactions. By safeguarding our inner peace, we ensure our balance and well-being, regardless of external tumult.

"Tension is who you think you should be. Relaxation is who you are."

Chinese Proverb

This age-old Chinese wisdom hints at the societal pressures and self-imposed expectations that often become sources of stress. Authentic relaxation and well-being arise when we embrace our true selves, letting go of the masks and facades we think we should wear.

"Your hand opens and closes, opens and closes. If it were always a fist or always stretched open, you would be paralyzed. Your deepest presence is in every small contracting and expanding, the two as beautifully balanced and coordinated as birds' wings."

Rumi

The Sufi poet Rumi uses the hand's motions as a metaphor for life's cyclical nature. There are times for action and times for rest, moments to grasp opportunities and moments to let go. Recognizing and flowing with these cycles ensures a harmonious existence.

Conclusion

Through the lens of these timeless quotes, we gain insights into the intricate dance of balance and well-being. In the midst of life's oscillations, these words serve as anchors, guiding us towards a centered existence. They remind us of the simple truths: that in balance lies the essence of a fulfilling life, and in well-being lies the essence of true richness. Embracing these principles enables us to navigate life's waves with grace, poise, and a profound sense of inner peace.

Practical Tips for Maintaining Balance

In our fast-paced modern world, the concept of balance often feels elusive. With increasing demands on our time from work, family, and societal commitments, finding equilibrium can seem like a Herculean task. However, achieving and maintaining balance is paramount for our well-being, productivity, and overall quality of life. This comprehensive guide will walk you through practical strategies that can help you tread the tightrope of modern living with grace and poise.

Prioritize Self-awareness:

Understanding Yourself

Before you can establish balance, you need to understand what balance looks like for you. This involves deep introspection to discern your values, priorities, and non-negotiables.

Regular Check-ins

Regularly ask yourself how you're feeling. Overwhelmed? Exhausted? Inspired? These feelings can serve as indicators, pointing to areas of your life that may need attention.

Set Clear Boundaries

Work-life Divide

Define strict start and end times for your workday. Resist the urge to check emails or work outside these hours.

Learn to Say 'No'

It's okay to decline invitations or requests that don't align with your current priorities. Overcommitting leads to burnout and imbalance.

Time Management and Planning

Prioritize Tasks

Not everything that demands your attention deserves it. Classify tasks based on urgency and importance.

Use Tools

Make use of planners, digital calendars, or apps like Trello and Todoist to organize your day.

Time-blocking

Allocate specific blocks of time for different activities. This helps ensure that all facets of your life get the attention they deserve.

Embrace Flexibility

Adjust and Adapt

Life is unpredictable. Sometimes, despite our best plans, things go awry. Instead of rigidly sticking to a plan, adjust as needed.

Re-evaluate Regularly

Your definition of balance might change over time. Make it a habit to reassess your priorities and strategies periodically.

Physical Well-being

Regular Exercise

Physical activity is not just for physical health; it plays a key role in mental well-being and maintaining balance.

Nutrition

A balanced diet fuels both the body and mind, ensuring you have the energy to tackle your day.

Rest

Prioritize sleep. A well-rested mind and body are more efficient, focused, and balanced.

Mental and Emotional Self-care

Mindfulness and Meditation

These practices anchor you to the present moment, helping combat the stresses of modern life.

Seek Support

Talk to friends, family, or professionals when feeling overwhelmed. Sharing burdens lightens the load.

Engage in Hobbies

Pursuing passions outside of work provides relaxation and a break from routine.

Digital Detox

Set Limits

Allocate specific times when you will stay away from digital devices.

Unplug Before Bed

The blue light from screens can interfere with sleep. Aim for at least an hour of screen-free time before bed.

Notifications

Turn off non-essential notifications. They can fragment your focus, making it hard to maintain balance.

Create a Supportive Environment

Declutter

A clutter-free environment reduces anxiety and promotes focus.

Surround Yourself with Positivity

Engage with supportive friends and family, consume uplifting content, and consider joining groups or communities that share your goals or values.

Set Personal Goals

Short-term and Long-term

While long-term goals provide direction, short-term goals offer motivation and a sense of achievement.

Review and Reset

Periodically assess your progress. If goals no longer align with your vision of balance, don't hesitate to adjust them.

Celebrate Achievements

Acknowledge Wins

Every step, no matter how small, towards balance should be celebrated.

Avoid Comparison

Your balance might look different from someone else's. Celebrate your unique journey without comparing it to others.

Conclusion

Maintaining balance in life is not a destination but an ongoing journey. It requires constant reflection, adaptation, and commitment. In this multifaceted journey, every individual's path is unique. What brings balance to one person might not work for another. The key lies in understanding oneself, setting clear priorities, and making conscious choices every day. By implementing these practical strategies, you can navigate the complexities of modern life with confidence, ensuring a harmonious blend of productivity, fulfillment, and well-being. Remember, balance is not about perfection but about making consistent efforts to create a life that resonates with your core values and aspirations.

Chapter 10
Legacy & Impact

The concept of legacy transcends the mere idea of tangible assets passed on after one's time. Instead, it dives deep into the realms of impact, influence, and the imprint one leaves behind – both in the world of business and in personal spheres. How will you be remembered? What difference have you made? This chapter delves into understanding legacy, its importance in the realm of business success, and the ways one can shape and nurture their lasting impact.

The Essence of Legacy

Defining Legacy

Going beyond the traditional definitions, legacy encapsulates the lasting effects of one's actions, decisions, and leadership. It is the story that outlives the storyteller.

Beyond the Tangible

While physical assets and financial bequests are aspects of one's legacy, the intangible – values, principles, and teachings – often resonate more deeply and last longer.

Why Legacy Matters in Business

Branding Beyond Products: A company's legacy is tightly knit with its brand image. How it treats its employees, its ethos, and its contributions to society all shape its lasting impression.

Attracting Talent

A strong legacy attracts potential employees who align with the company's values and vision.

Customer Loyalty

Businesses that emphasize ethical dealings and positive community impact often enjoy a dedicated and loyal customer base.

Building a Lasting Business Legacy

Ethical Foundations

Base business decisions on a strong ethical foundation. This includes fair trade practices, ethical sourcing, and transparent dealings.

Value-Driven Leadership

Leaders should operate from a place of value and principle, emphasizing the importance of leaving a positive mark.

Community Engagement

Actively engage with the community, be it through charitable work, supporting local events, or sustainability initiatives.

Personal Legacy in the Business World

Personal Branding

How business leaders present themselves, their personal ethos, and their engagement outside of business affairs all contribute to their personal legacy.

Continuous Learning and Growth

Emphasizing personal development, attending seminars, reading widely, and pursuing further educational endeavors can shape one's lasting impression.

Networking and Relationships

Building genuine, meaningful relationships in the business world can have long-term repercussions. These relationships often outlive professional engagements.

Impact: The Legacy Catalyst

Quantifying Impact

Understanding the measurable change, be it in the form of societal contributions, environmental efforts, or workplace culture shifts, can provide clarity on legacy direction.

Qualitative Impact

Delving into the more intangible effects, like shifts in industry standards, influencing peers, or changing consumer perceptions, provides a comprehensive view of one's impact.

Succession Planning

Grooming Future Leaders

Legacy is also about ensuring that the business or venture thrives beyond one's active involvement. Preparing the next generation of leaders is crucial.

Knowledge Transfer

A systematic approach to passing on knowledge, experiences, and insights ensures that the company's ethos and values continue to thrive.

Overcoming Legacy Challenges

Adapting to Change

Businesses and leaders must be agile, adapting to evolving market scenarios while staying true to their core values.

Facing Criticism

Constructive feedback is invaluable for growth. However, it's essential to differentiate between constructive criticism and baseless negativity.

Legacy Stories: Inspiring Examples from the Business World

Case Study 1

A deep dive into a renowned business leader's journey, emphasizing their lasting impact on the industry and society.

Case Study 2

An exploration of a corporation's evolution, the values it upheld, and its lasting legacy in its sector.

Nurturing Your Legacy

Reflection and Introspection

Regularly assess the impact you're making. Are your actions aligned with the legacy you wish to leave?

Mentorship

Actively mentoring younger professionals not only contributes to their growth but solidifies your impact and legacy.

Conclusion

Leaving a legacy is about living with purpose and intentionality. In the business realm, this translates to making decisions that not only benefit the bottom line but also positively impact society, employees, and the broader industry. True legacy transcends time, surviving market fluctuations, management changes, and evolving business models. It is immortalized in the lives touched, the standards set, and the positive change instigated. By understanding, valuing, and actively shaping one's legacy, business professionals ensure that their influence remains long after they've stepped away from the boardroom.

Beyond the Bottom Line:Rethinking Business Success

For decades, the success of a business was evaluated predominantly through its financial metrics – profit margins, revenue growth, shareholder value, and so on. However, as the global business environment evolves, the definition of success is undergoing a transformative shift. It's not just about profit anymore. Businesses today recognize the significance of broader societal, environmental, and ethical impacts. "Beyond the Bottom Line" delves into this expansive understanding of success and how modern enterprises are redefining their roles in a rapidly changing world.

Understanding the Traditional Bottom Line

To appreciate the shift, one must first understand the traditional concept of the bottom line. In its classical sense, the bottom line refers to the net profit or loss of a company, found at the 'bottom' of its income statement. This number has historically been the single most important figure for businesses, dictating decisions, strategies, and more.

The Advent of the Triple Bottom Line

The term "Triple Bottom Line" (TBL) was coined by John Elkington in 1994. TBL expanded the singular focus from pure profit (economic bottom line) to include environmental and social considerations. These three pillars – profit, planet, and people – advocate for a more holistic approach to business success.

Profit

Still remains a primary concern but isn't the exclusive focus. Profit enables sustainability and growth, but other factors are equally valued.

Planet

Recognizes the environmental responsibility of businesses. From carbon footprint to sustainable sourcing, it emphasizes ecological consciousness in corporate decisions.

People

Focuses on social responsibility. This can range from ethical labor practices to community outreach and development.

Why the Shift Matters

The Changing Business Landscape

Several factors have contributed to this broader perspective on business success:

Informed Consumers

With the digital age, consumers are more informed about corporate practices. They often make buying decisions based on a company's ethical, environmental, and social standings.

Sustainable Development Goals (SDGs)

Global initiatives, like the United Nations' SDGs, emphasize the collective responsibility of sectors, including business, in achieving a sustainable future.

Long-term Viability

Companies recognize that sustainable and ethical practices often align with long-term success and risk mitigation.

Case Studies

Going Beyond the Traditional

Patagonia

This outdoor clothing brand has made environmental consciousness a core part of its business model, from using sustainable materials to actively promoting environmental causes.

Ben & Jerry's

Beyond just ice cream, the company is known for its social advocacy, fair trade practices, and community-centric initiatives.

Challenges in Expanding the Definition of Success

Broadening the scope of success isn't without its challenges

Balancing Profit with Other Priorities

It's a delicate act to ensure that while focusing on environmental and social aspects, the business remains financially viable.

Measuring Impact

Unlike clear financial metrics, gauging social or environmental impact can be more abstract.

Stakeholder Resistance

Traditional investors or stakeholders might be resistant to this broader understanding, primarily if short-term profits are impacted.

The Future:Beyond Even the Triple Bottom Line

As businesses become more intertwined with global challenges, there's a push to consider even broader criteria

Technological Responsibility

With the rise of AI and data analytics, businesses are being held accountable for their technological choices, especially around user privacy and ethical AI.

Cultural Impact

Companies, especially global giants, play a role in shaping cultures. Their influence in promoting inclusivity, diversity, and positive cultural shifts is now under the microscope.

In Conclusion: A New Paradigm

The redefinition of business success is not a fleeting trend. It reflects the evolving role of businesses in a globalized, interconnected world. While profit remains essential, the broader impacts of a company's actions on the environment, society, culture, and even technology are becoming non-negotiable aspects of their legacy. In understanding and embracing this shift, businesses are not just aiming for financial prosperity but a lasting, positive imprint on the world.

Inspiring Quotes on Legacy: More than Footprints in the Sands of Time

The word 'legacy' carries with it an inherent weight and sense of permanence. More than just the material assets one leaves behind, a legacy encapsulates the lasting impact an individual or entity imprints on the world. Philosophers, leaders, and thinkers throughout history have contemplated the essence of legacy. Their words offer guidance, introspection, and motivation. This chapter delves into some of the most inspiring quotes on legacy and unravels their deeper meanings and implications.

"Legacy is not leaving something for people. It's leaving something in people."

- *Peter Strople*

Interpretation

Peter Strople's insight reminds us that true legacy is not about tangible assets. Rather, it's about the values, lessons, and memories instilled within individuals. For businesses, this could mean fostering a corporate culture that prioritizes ethics over profits, or for individuals, it might imply nurturing and mentoring the next generation.

"Carve your name on hearts, not tombstones. A legacy is etched into the minds of others and the stories they share about you."

- *Shannon L. Alder*

Interpretation

Alder's words underscore the ephemeral nature of material possessions and achievements. Tombstones erode, but memories and stories are passed down through generations. This quote emphasizes the importance of personal relationships and genuine connections.

"Our days are numbered. One of the primary goals in our lives should be to prepare for our last day. The legacy we leave is not just in our possessions, but in the quality of our lives."

- *Billy Graham*

Interpretation

Billy Graham, a renowned evangelist, touches upon the transient nature of life. His words serve as a reminder that the real measure of a life well-lived isn't in the wealth accumulated, but in the positive influences and changes we bring about during our time.

"The things you do for yourself are gone when you are gone, but the things you do for others remain as your legacy."

- Kalu Ndukwe Kalu

Interpretation

Acts of selflessness and contributions to the collective good are the true markers of a lasting legacy. Kalu Ndukwe Kalu emphasizes the importance of altruism and the difference one can make in the lives of others.

"You can't leave a legacy behind if you're always worried about tomorrow. If you want to leave a legacy, work really hard, be kind, and you can figure everything else out."

- Jonah Green

Interpretation

Jonah Green's perspective sheds light on the balance between planning for the future and living in the moment. To leave a legacy, one must be present, engaged, and dedicated to their craft or cause, without being paralyzed by anxieties of the future.

"To leave a legacy, you don't have to be rich, famous, or powerful. You just have to touch people's lives in such a way that you're never forgotten."

- Unknown

Interpretation

This quote demystifies the concept of legacy, making it accessible to everyone. It underscores the fact that everyday acts of kindness, compassion, and understanding can have lasting impacts.

"What you leave behind is not what is engraved in stone monuments, but what is woven into the lives of others."

- Pericles

Interpretation

The ancient Athenian leader Pericles delves into the impermanent nature of physical monuments versus the lasting nature of influences on individuals. It's a nod to the importance of personal legacies over grand gestures.

"Your story is the greatest legacy that you will leave to your friends. It's the longest-lasting legacy you will leave to your heirs."

- Steve Saint

Interpretation

Steve Saint reminds us that our personal narratives, filled with struggles, triumphs, failures, and learnings, are valuable lessons for those who come after us. Sharing these stories ensures that they continue to inspire and educate for generations.

Conclusion

Legacy, as reflected in these quotes, is an intricate tapestry of our actions, influences, and narratives. It's the indelible mark we leave on the world and people around us. While material assets may fade, the stories, values, and changes we bring about are the true essence of our legacy. As we navigate our personal and professional journeys, these quotes serve as beacons, guiding us toward a path of purpose, meaning, and lasting impact.

Making a Lasting Difference in Business and Beyond

In the corporate landscape, businesses emerge, evolve, and sometimes even dissolve. Yet, some businesses leave an indelible mark not just within their industry but in society at large. They do so not just through profitability or market dominance, but through their principles, ethos, and commitment to making a difference. The true essence of a lasting difference transcends quarterly earnings and dives into the realms of societal impact, ethical governance, and a sustainable vision.

The Pillars of a Purpose-Driven Business

Defining Purpose

Today's corporate giants like Patagonia, Ben & Jerry's, and TOMS Shoes don't just sell products; they sell a vision. These companies have identified a larger purpose than merely profit-making. Whether it's sustainability, fair trade, or philanthropy, they anchor their operations around a defined mission.

Integrity and Transparency

Authenticity can't be faked. Companies that genuinely prioritize a social cause or ethical practices ensure that these principles permeate every layer of their operations. This involves being transparent about sourcing, production processes, or even their profit margins.

Ethical Governance: Going Beyond Compliance

Regulations set the minimum standards, but businesses that aspire to make a genuine difference often exceed these benchmarks. They adopt practices that might be costlier or less efficient in the short term, but yield long-term societal benefits.

For example, while many corporations might adhere to the minimum environmental standards set by regulations, companies making a lasting difference would adopt environmentally friendly practices even when not mandated, be it through carbon neutrality initiatives or waste reduction programs.

Employee Empowerment and Welfare

A Fair Workplace

Making a difference isn't just about external initiatives. It starts from within. Businesses that leave a mark ensure their workplaces are diverse, inclusive, and foster growth. This means fair pay, opportunities for continuous learning, and an environment where every voice is heard.

Beyond the Paycheck

Some companies have embedded employee welfare into their core principles. They offer benefits like extended parental leave, mental health resources, or even stock options. This not only boosts morale but ensures that employees are stakeholders in the company's broader vision.

Community Engagement and Grassroots Impact

Many companies adopt Corporate Social Responsibility (CSR) initiatives, but those making a substantial impact often go a step further. They engage with communities, understand their needs, and tailor initiatives accordingly. Instead of sporadic charity events, they develop sustained programs that aim for long-term upliftment.

For instance, companies might partner with local schools to enhance education, work with NGOs to tackle societal issues, or even foster entrepreneurship within marginalized communities.

Sustainable Growth and Environmental Stewardship

In today's climate-conscious world, businesses can't afford to ignore their environmental footprint. But beyond this reactive approach lies a proactive strategy: embedding sustainability into the business model.

Green Innovation

Companies making a lasting impact often invest in R&D to create greener products or solutions. This isn't just about being eco-friendly; it's about pioneering innovations that set industry benchmarks.

Supply Chain Sustainability: From sourcing raw materials to transportation logistics, companies are ensuring that every step is as green and ethical as possible.

The Ripple Effect: Inspiring Others

Companies that have made a tangible difference often inspire others to follow suit. Their legacy lies not just in their direct impact but in the standards they set for their peers. By leading by example, they create a ripple effect, nudging the entire industry towards more ethical and impactful practices.

Building a Legacy: Long-term Vision over Short-term Gains

Lasting impact requires patience and persistence. The most influential companies aren't swayed by short-term market pressures. Instead, they remain committed to their vision, even if it means sacrificing immediate profitability. They recognize that true value isn't just in stock prices but in societal impact and the legacy they leave behind.

Conclusion

Making a lasting difference in the world of business is a journey, not a destination. It requires an unwavering commitment to a larger purpose, a genuine desire to create positive change, and the tenacity to persevere through challenges. Businesses that manage to embed these principles within their DNA not only thrive commercially but elevate their stature from mere commercial entities to influential institutions in society. Their legacy then becomes a beacon for others, illustrating that success in business and making a positive difference are not mutually exclusive but can, in fact, go hand in hand.

Conclusion
The Harmonious Intersection of Business and Impact

In the dynamic realm of the corporate world, success is often measured in profit margins, stock prices, and market shares. Yet, as we've journeyed through the different facets of business in our exploration, a larger truth emerges: The most influential and enduring businesses are those that prioritize a purpose beyond profitability. This purpose, rooted deeply in values, ethics, and a desire to foster positive change, becomes the compass that guides their decisions and the beacon that illuminates their legacy.

The Changing Corporate Paradigm

Historically, the business realm was defined largely by its quest for profits. Capitalist ventures, by design, sought to maximize shareholder value. However, as societies evolved, so did their expectations from businesses. Communities began looking beyond the products or services a company offered; they started valuing the ethos behind the brand, the principles guiding its operations, and the footprint it left on the world.

In this new paradigm, businesses are not just economic entities; they are influential agents of societal change. Their reach, resources, and influence position them uniquely to address pressing global challenges, from environmental sustainability to social inequities. Companies like Patagonia in sustainable fashion, Tesla in clean energy, and Unilever with its Sustainable Living Plan exemplify this shift. They underscore the principle that economic success and societal impact can coexist, even amplify each other.

The Role of Leadership

The transition from a purely profit-driven approach to one anchored in purpose often starts at the helm. Visionary leaders recognize that in the long run, aligning with societal values and needs doesn't detract from a company's success; it augments it. They understand that today's consumers, especially the younger generation, resonate with brands that stand for something, that wear their values on their sleeves and embed them in their actions. These leaders are not just business strategists; they're change-makers, pioneering a corporate landscape where ethics, impact, and profitability intersect harmoniously.

The Community and Employee Dynamic

While external impact is pivotal, the internal corporate environment is equally significant. Businesses that strive for a lasting legacy understand the importance of nurturing their most valuable asset: their employees. They foster workplaces where diversity is celebrated, where every voice matters, and where growth is not just a corporate aim but an individual pursuit. Such businesses recognize that when employees are aligned with the company's vision and values, they become its most potent ambassadors, driving both its commercial and societal objectives.

Moreover, these corporations don't operate in silos. They engage deeply with the communities they serve, adopting a stakeholder-centric approach rather than a purely shareholder-driven one. Through such engagement, they understand grassroots challenges and tailor solutions accordingly, ensuring their initiatives are relevant, effective, and sustainable.

Legacy Beyond Business Metrics

The true measure of a business's impact isn't confined to its balance sheets. It's reflected in the positive changes it catalyzes, the standards it sets for its peers, and the legacy it carves in the annals of corporate history. It's seen in the lives uplifted through its initiatives, the environmental disasters averted through its sustainable practices, and the societal norms challenged through its progressive stance.

Looking Forward: The Future of Business

As we envision the future, one thing becomes clear: The businesses that will thrive and be celebrated will be those that operate at the nexus of success and significance. They will innovate not just to capture markets, but to address societal challenges. They will strategize not just for quarterly growth, but for generational impact. They will exist not just to sell, but to serve.

In this future, every business decision will be a reflection of a deeper purpose, every corporate initiative an embodiment of a cherished value. Profit, while still crucial, will be one of the many metrics of success, and businesses will be revered not just for their commercial prowess but for their role as torchbearers of positive change.

As we conclude, let's remember: In the boardroom and beyond, the true essence of business success lies not just in the wealth it accumulates but in the difference it makes. It's in the legacy it leaves, echoing in the annals of time, inspiring generations to come.

Reflecting on the Journey: A Tapestry of Insights, Aspirations, and Transformations

The journey of exploring the multifaceted world of business, as delineated in this book, has been akin to navigating through a labyrinth of wisdom, experiences, and evolutionary shifts. As we pause to reflect on this odyssey, it's essential to distill the profound lessons, appreciate the transitional phases, and project our aspirations for a harmonious confluence of business practices and human values.

The Dance of Dichotomies

At the heart of our exploration lies the ever-present tension between profit and purpose, between individual ambition and collective wellbeing. The corporate world, historically profit-centric, has been in a transformative dance, oscillating between these dichotomies. The most heartening observation is the increasing realization that these dichotomies aren't mutually exclusive. Businesses today are increasingly proving that purpose can drive profit, and individual ambition can fuel collective upliftment.

The Resonance of Quotes

This book employed the profound power of quotes to convey complex ideas succinctly. These timeless words serve as beacons, illuminating the path forward. They encapsulate the wisdom of ages and the insights of luminaries. Each quote, carefully chosen, served as a pause, prompting introspection and reevaluation, enabling us to align our actions with overarching principles.

Leadership's Transformative Power

One of the most salient takeaways has been the role of visionary leadership in redirecting the ship of business. Leaders, with their far-reaching influence, have the unique capability to redefine objectives, align teams, and initiate ripple effects that can change entire industries. The leaders we discussed, through their actions and philosophies, showcased how a purpose-driven approach could revolutionize business landscapes.

Valuing Human Capital

A recurring theme was the indomitable value of people – be it as consumers, employees, or stakeholders. Businesses that understand, value, and nurture their human capital tend to not only succeed but also endure. From fostering collaboration and teamwork to promoting personal growth and wellbeing, the spotlight on the human aspect of business was relentless and rightly so.

Ethical Grounding as a Non-Negotiable

The chapters on ethics and integrity highlighted that the bedrock of any successful business venture should be its moral compass. With an increasingly interconnected world and a discerning consumer base, businesses that sidestep ethical considerations face not just economic repercussions but also eroded trust and tainted legacies.

Embracing Change and Challenges

The sections on innovation, creativity, and resilience underscored the need to embrace change – be it in the form of market shifts, technological advancements, or unforeseen challenges. The business world is not static. Those who adapt, innovate, and derive lessons from setbacks emerge as frontrunners, setting benchmarks for others to follow.

The Vitality of Clear Communication

Without clear and effective communication, even the most revolutionary ideas risk obscurity. Our discussions on communication and influence reiterated the importance of crafting resonant messages, understanding one's audience, and leveraging influence responsibly to inspire action.

Legacy – The Ultimate Business KPI

Conventional business metrics like ROI, market share, and annual growth are vital. However, the chapters on legacy and impact drove home the point that the ultimate key performance indicator (KPI) of a business is the lasting difference it makes in the world. Profitability might determine a business's success in the short run, but its legacy ascertains its place in history.

The Road Ahead

While our journey through these pages concludes, the larger journey for businesses worldwide continues. The future beckons with its array of challenges and opportunities. The blueprint, however, remains clear: A blend of unwavering ethical grounding, visionary leadership, and a genuine commitment to value all stakeholders.

In wrapping up, this journey through "In the Boardroom & Beyond" hasn't been a mere academic exercise. It has been an invitation to introspect, to challenge status quo thinking, to dream of a world where business success and societal well-being thrive in tandem. As we step forward, armed with these insights, let's pledge to be the harbingers of this change, to craft not just profitable enterprises, but impactful legacies. Let this reflection serve as both a culmination of our present explorations and the prologue to many more transformative journeys ahead.

The Future of Business Success: A Blend of Innovation, Ethics, and Human-Centric Approaches

The ever-evolving landscape of business continually prompts industry leaders, analysts, and pioneers to ponder the question: "What does the future of business success look like?" Looking ahead, it is evident that the traditional metrics of profitability and growth, while still crucial, are no longer the sole determinants of success. The future pivots on a multifaceted approach that encompasses innovation, ethical practices, and a human-centric mindset.

Innovation at the Forefront

In the age of rapid technological advancements, the capacity to innovate has become a significant pillar of business success. Whether it's integrating Artificial Intelligence (AI) in decision-making processes, leveraging the Internet of Things (IoT) to enhance customer experience, or harnessing big data analytics to glean business insights, companies that are agile and willing to embrace and invest in new technologies are positioned at the vanguard of their industries.

Yet, innovation isn't confined to technology alone. It extends to business models, strategies, and company cultures. Take, for instance, the rise of subscription-based models across various sectors or the push towards a circular economy, emphasizing sustainability and resource maximization. Businesses that can think outside the box, challenging conventional norms, and trailblazing new paths will define success in the future.

Unwavering Commitment to Ethics

The increased emphasis on corporate social responsibility (CSR) and the surge of conscious consumerism underline a shifting paradigm. Customers are no longer just seeking quality products or services but are progressively aligning with brands that resonate with their values. As a result, companies that operate transparently, take a stance on global issues, and are environmentally conscious will find a competitive edge.

Moreover, with platforms like social media acting as watchdogs, holding corporations accountable, ethical missteps can result in severe reputational damage, eroding trust and affecting the bottom line. Consequently, ethics is no longer a mere checkbox but a cornerstone of future business success.

Putting People First

The human element remains at the heart of business. As automation and AI take on more roles within organizations, the need to emphasize soft skills – like emotional intelligence, critical thinking, and creativity – becomes paramount. The future of business success will rely on leaders who can cultivate a culture of continuous learning, empathy, and collaboration.

Additionally, the recent global events, like the COVID-19 pandemic, have spotlighted the importance of employee well-being, flexibility, and mental health support in the workplace. Companies that prioritize their employees' holistic well-being will benefit from increased loyalty, productivity, and a positive brand image.

Furthermore, the businesses of the future will need to be attuned to changing consumer needs, emphasizing personalization, and fostering genuine relationships. In an increasingly digital world, human touch and authentic connections will be treasured commodities.

Diversity and Inclusion as Strengths

Future business success will be shaped by organizations that understand the power of diverse perspectives. The push for more inclusive workplaces, which welcome individuals regardless of their gender, race, age, or background, isn't just a moral imperative but a business one. Diverse teams are proven to be more creative, innovative, and better problem solvers, reflecting a broader customer base and tapping into global markets more effectively.

Resilience and Adaptability

In a volatile, uncertain, complex, and ambiguous (VUCA) world, the businesses that thrive will be those that exhibit resilience and adaptability. Whether it's navigating economic downturns, adjusting to industry disruptions, or mitigating unforeseen challenges, companies that are built to endure and pivot when necessary will define the future.

Conclusion

The future of business success paints a picture of a world where companies operate at the intersection of profit and purpose. By intertwining innovation, ethics, and a human-centric approach, businesses won't just thrive; they will lead, setting benchmarks for global good while achieving unprecedented success. As we steer into this future, the onus is on today's leaders to craft visions that are inclusive, forward-thinking, and anchored in values that resonate with a global audience.